THE
ART OF SALES
MARKETING & THE SPOKESPERSON

HOW OVER A 100 MILLION
GEORGE FOREMAN GRILLS WERE SOLD

Leon Dreimann and Samantha Dreimann

Foreword by George Foreman

First published 2015
Copyright © Leon Dreimann and Samantha Dreimann 2015.
ISBN: 978-0692453810

Contents

FOREWORD

I have often heard it said, "There are two sides to every story." Maybe so, if someone got the facts wrong.

But for the first time things are lined up just right, and the truth of the matter is right here.

What happens when the ultimate entrepreneur meets one of the world's best knockout salespeople, then teams up with a great bunch of 24/7 give-all-your-heart-workers, all with one dream in common? To have the whole world scream, "The Lean Mean Fat Reducing Grilling Machine!"

Yes we did it. Leon Dreimann assembled a cast of characters, armed with honesty, integrity and belief in a leader who was fearless in business; we made it happen.

Read and take this journey with us. You too might be inspired to make the world sing your song.

In this book you will see that all things are possible.

George Foreman
Houston, 2014

A STRANGE ASSIGNMENT

It was suggested to me to write one or two pages to tell readers who I am. Sounds easy, doesn't it? But at my age, telling a story about who I am now, and the progression of growing into the me of today, may need a thousand pages. Perhaps another book? I'll tell you just enough here, the stuff about me that matters in relation to this book.

I am the guy that put George Foreman and a grill together. How? This book will tell you. My background took me from sales, to management, to marketing and to a position as CEO of a publicly-held company, all in the field of consumer products. Along the way I found out that my strengths developed when I did things I loved.

After winning Salesman of the Year at Gillette, a promotion took me to management and then combined management with product marketing. I really enjoyed good products and especially innovation.

You need entrepreneurial drive and skills, as well as a large amount of creativity to get innovation recognized and accepted by consumers. You need courage and confidence to take risks and not accept failure at the end of it all. I really loved it when everybody would say, "this will not work" and have our team prove them wrong.

Failure to me was a signal to look for another way to succeed. As CEO, I took lessons learned from the many talented people I worked with over the years as well as the experience from past positions. I became a CEO of a company doing $8 million in sales, and, in a few years, we took in almost $1.4 billion. I am most proud of having the skill to find and put together a great team of people that were a pleasure to work with. They demonstrated skills when I found them and asked them to join our team. Then they took it up several notches by developing their skills and having the swagger of being a part of one of the most innovative teams ever.

That's what I looked for in a corporate team. You know what I looked for in a spokesperson? The same thing: drive, honesty, love of innovation, intelligence and a big huge smile.

Boy, did a boxer named George Foreman fit that bill.

PART I:

GEORGE, THE MAN

BY LEON DREIMANN

Many things have been written and documented about George and his achievements. What I want to introduce to you is George and his many other facets, aspects of the man rarely discussed in the media, or by people mainly interested in George's history-making moments.

Yes, George was one of the best Heavy Weight Boxing Champions in the World. Yes, his charisma sold over 100 million George Foreman Grills, as well as many other great products.

However, over the years travelling with George, making store and media appearances in promoting the George Foreman Grills, I witnessed many surprising and wonderful moments. I became increasingly impressed with George's character, his intelligence, perseverance, humbleness, love for all mankind and especially youth in need of his guidance and example.

It was always clear George's competence and talent gave him a great chance to succeed in anything he put his mind to, a champion in everything he does. Even now, he wins big. Check out these recent photos from September 2013, of George winning a trophy with his beautiful dog Abelle, at a show in Germany.

Images provided by George Foreman

George worked his way up from the bottom and did well as Champion of the World, Super Salesman and a great family man. But if he wanted to be a brain surgeon, a scholar, or a politician, there is no doubt in my mind he would have been the best at anything he wanted to be.

Having spent more than 20 years with George as a partner and friend, I believe the sayings "if at first you don't succeed, try, try again", "just do it," and "believe," describe George 100% and are a part of his huge success.

George can tell jokes when dealing with the media, fans, family and friends; usually about himself. But when people stop asking him questions about boxing or the grill and approach a different subject, they will find George to be well-read, well educated in current affairs and often deeply insightful into many subjects that bring an idea into a new light and likely have you agreeing with his conclusions.

He was asked one time about what he thought of Muhammad Ali. George's response was about how he admired the man for being the first major sports personality willing to put his entire career in jeopardy by expressing unpopular opinions, to say the least. He became a Muslim and changed his name from Cassius Clay to Muhammad Ali, was willing to go to jail for being a conscientious objector to the war in Vietnam, and was not allowed to fight for over 3 years. These actions were even more history-making than his boxing career.

No sporting great until that time was as outspoken and influential in matters outside the sport they were known for. When hearing George talk about Ali, you understood that Ali was not just a great boxer, he was a man in our history. George keeps in touch with Ali, and they have a wonderful relationship. Both are legends and played a major part in each other's lives.

Shortly after 9/11, George and I were on our way to London for some promotions. Entering the plane George got a standing ovation all the way up and down the aisle. George is on board. "We are safe now!" were the cries; this was an amazing moment.

While travelling to London, George walked over to my seat and handed me a CD player with headphones. He said, "I have written some songs I plan to have recorded. Could you listen to them and let me know what you think?" My immediate reaction was… *you have to be kidding me*. George writing songs? Doesn't he know there are thousands of talented people in the music industry that never get a chance? But I put the headphones on and pressed play. After a few seconds of listening to some beautiful peaceful music played by a symphony orchestra with a wonderful choir and tenor, I stopped the CD and went over to George's seat and told him he gave me the wrong CD. What's in the player is some classical music he must have been listening to. "No", he told me, "this is the right CD. It's a demo. The Orchestra is the Vienna Festival Orchestra, the Choir is the Vienna Boys Choir and the tenor is Vargas." I was speechless.

Eventually, a double CD was released called *Inspirations*. There were many performers featured on this album; Aretha Franklin, the Vienna Boys Choir, Ramon Vargas, Jose Carreras, Michael Crawford, Jim Nabors and many more. There were different composers on the CD as well. But George got his music on an album.

I thought this was amazing. George simply said to himself, *I will write some songs and have them recorded*; then, he went out and found a way to get it done!

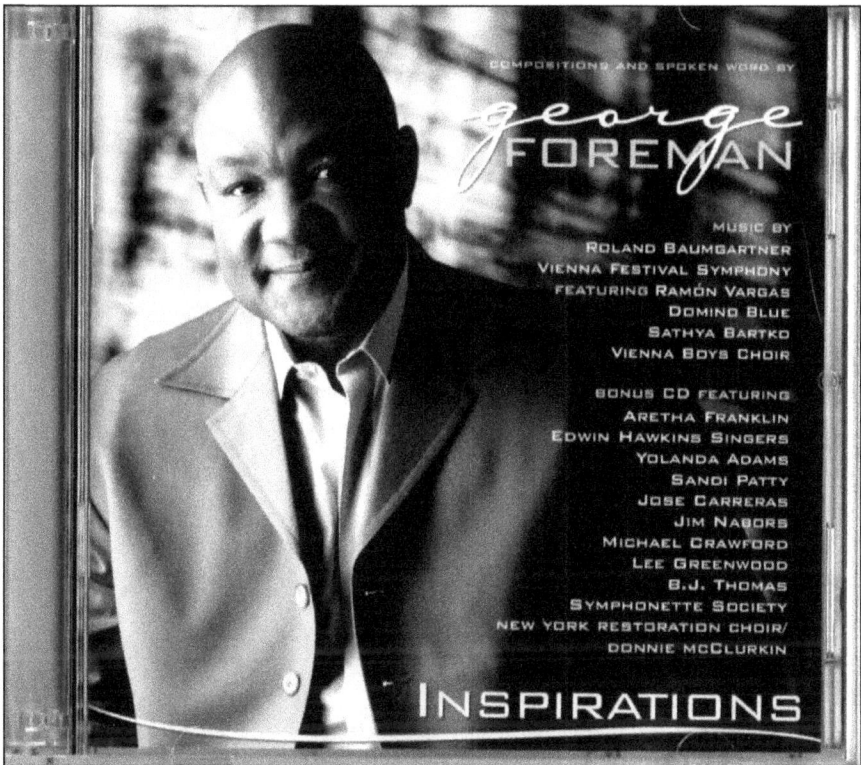

CD Cover: Inspirations

Another time George told me he had written a children's book. It will be out soon, he said. Again I held my breath. A children's book? Sometime later the book came out and I was sent a review, published in the *New York Times*. When I started reading the review, I held my breath and my heart rate increased immediately.

The review was great. George had another success.

Here is the review: **http://bit.ly/NYTimesLGDO**

Publisher: Simon & Schuster Children's Publishing (April 26, 2005)

Then there was everything from a movie role, a family reality show, boxing commentary for HBO, TV show appearances with Jay Leno to being a judge on *American Inventor*.

The November, 1994 *Sports Illustrated* showed George on the cover boxing Michael Moore in the fight where he regained the Heavyweight Championship title at age 45.

By December, 1995, *Forbes* had George on the cover sporting his boxing gloves, a scowl on his face, and the headline *Businessman George Foreman "I'm not the greatest boxer, but I'm the greatest salesman in the world."*

In June of 2003, a *Fortune Small Business* cover with George in a shirt and tie, striking a boxing pose with a twinkle in his eyes, announced, *"The Foreman Magic. A small grill company used the champ to create a killer brand. Can other celebs do the same for you?"*

George supports many charities he believes in. One effort he is very proud of is *The George Foreman Youth & Community Center*. He built it in 1984 in Houston with money he had saved through his eight-year retirement. He wanted to create a haven for kids to hang out. His comeback to boxing, that World Heavy Weight Championship title at the age of 45, was necessary when he ran out of money to support this center.

Rather than go out to raise money from others, he put on his trunks and went out and earned it himself. His reward? Another Heavyweight Boxing Championship of the World win at the age of 45!

George bearing gifts, at Foreman Youth & Community Center.
http://www.georgeforeman.com/youth_center

George received a humanitarian award from the Aids Foundation Houston's Stone Soup Pantry and an honoree doctorate from the Houston Graduate School of Theology for his charity work with children.

He has been an ordained minister for over 20 years and preaches in *"The Church of Lord Jesus Christ"* in Houston. For all of the promotional activities or appearances planned with George, he had only one request of us and that was that he had to be back in Houston with his congregation on Sunday.

During a radio interview in Missouri, the show host asked questions about George the World Champion, The George Foreman Grill and his big family. There was lots of kidding around and it was a fun interview.

All of a sudden the host changed the subject and asked George what he thought about the state government considering stopping funds for sports programs in high schools; no more football, baseball or basketball subsidies. The host went on to say that since funds were running out, focusing on education and letting the parents provide sports activities for the kids was not a bad idea. What did George think about this?

George was there to promote the Grill. Getting serious and talking politics is not a good business idea. So I sat up with interest to see how he would handle this.

George did get serious. He said it was a terrible idea. In school sports, children learn to be on a team. When playing sport on a team you learn to work together with other children from all walks of life, economic status, scholastic abilities and more. The team has one uniform. The rest of their adult life will depend on how they, as adults, handle their life working with others, interacting with neighbors, raising a family and working with peers, bosses and employees; many different teams striving to achieve various goals. Where else can our children learn and experience to do this, if not in school team sports?

That was the short version of George's passionate contribution to this radio show, but you get the idea. It took the host a few seconds after George finished to say anything. Then he said, "Wow, George how right you are!"

In the mid-nineties, I attended the Bakersfield conference held in the world's largest tent. Some of the many guest speakers included; George Bush, Margaret Thatcher, General Norman Schwarzkopf, Bob Hope and many other powerful, influential and successful men and women. Many held the highest office in various countries around the world, were business leaders of multi-national corporations, and Nobel Peace Prizewinners, among others. You get the idea. One of the speakers, you guessed it, was George Foreman.

I was nervous for George and hoped he would do well amongst this group of professional public speakers. When George finished he was one of three people to receive a standing ovation from the 9000 people in attendance. (Margaret Thatcher and Bob Hope were the other two.) I was so proud for him. It was a spectacular moment.

I heard George consistently answer the question of his greatest moment in boxing, which was winning an Olympic Gold Medal. This was the 1968 Olympics where some athletes chose to wear a black glove on one hand and raise it in the air when receiving medals on the podium. George, however, received the world's attention and admiration for raising the American Flag.

As this book tells the story of the George Foreman Grill, you will hear more stories, but for now I hope you can understand why I love, admire and respect "George the Man."

I am proud to call him my friend.

Credit: Gary Davis Illustration

THE EARLY STEPS:
GETTING MY EXPERIENCE TO ENDORSE PRODUCTS WITH CELEBRITIES

The key ingredients in the success of *The George Foreman Lean Mean Fat Reducing Grilling Machine* were the product and George Foreman, but there were many other events, people, and experiences, that helped launch the grill.

My experiences with celebrities began in the early 1960's when I worked in one of the most successful restaurants in Melbourne, Australia, *The Purple Cow*. It had a cute slogan on signs, napkins and advertising for the restaurant, taken from a famous poem written by Frank Gelett Burgess in the 1890's:

I never saw a Purple Cow,
I never hope to see one;
But I can tell you, anyhow,
I'd rather see than be one

The restaurant was located in downtown Melbourne on the corner of Collins Street and Exhibition Street, almost next to the Southern Cross Hotel, the best place to stay in those years.

The Navy Club was nearby; fashion stores and Chinatown were two blocks away.

I started at the Purple Cow as a dishwasher. After a few days, the owner, Victor, took a liking to me. He bought me a dinner suit with a shirt and bow tie and made me a waiter. A couple of months later, I was a "Jack of All Trades", going to the markets in the morning, buying produce, cooking on the grill, making salads, and doing the books. Victor gave me yet another salary increase and told all the staff I was now the Manager. I was earning $18 a week plus tips.

The restaurant owner's wife was an editor of *TV Week* Magazine. Every year, Melbourne had the TV *Logie's* and brought in celebrities from all over the world to attend, host and present trophies. The *Logie's* are similar to the *Emmy's* in the USA. Stories and photos would appear in the magazine about these stars. Almost always, the photos were shot in the *Purple Cow Restaurant* where they were dining. This was the main ingredient that made this restaurant hot. If it was good enough for the stars to eat there, *it must be good enough for you too*, was the message. This was my first lesson in "Star Power." If you want to compare it to something in the USA, think about Spago when it was on Sunset Boulevard in Hollywood, California from 1982 to 2001. Most of the regular customers included celebrities, such as movie stars, producers and politicians.

While managing the restaurant, I met some wonderful people and the experience stayed with me all my life. The most memorable meeting was the Beatles. With over 200,000 people camped outside their hotel, the Southern Cross, I assisted in sneaking them and a group of a dozen or more people out of the hotel. We took the back entrance of the hotel to the back entrance of our restaurant, which was only a few yards away. It was a Sunday night, June 14th, 1964, and our restaurant was closed to the public on Sundays; so the Beatles ate at the back of the restaurant, Victor the owner cooked and I served.

Few words were exchanged. I remember their accents and that they talked among themselves. I also remember how nervous we were that Melbourne fans would find out The Beatles were eating with us and storm the restaurant. It was a short meal. The group snuck back into a party at the hotel. I was not all that excited at the time. I was an Elvis fan and Beatniks and Rockers did not mix.

One bit of history is that the concert in Melbourne was the only time five Beatles played. Jimmy Nicol was hired as a temporary drummer when Ringo came down with tonsillitis. Ringo rejoined the group after a bout in a hospital on June 14th and Jimmy left the next day.

The Beatles can be seen in Madame Tussauds's wax Museum in London sculpted in their 1960s period of fame

While Beatle mania had started it was only the beginning of Beatle history. I had not yet turned 16 years old. Looking back now at video clips available online, boy oh boy, it was something. **http://bit.ly/BeatlesAU**

Another memory was spending time with the Englishman, Donald Campbell, over several weeks prior to him setting the world land speed record of 403.1 mph. When I met him, it was his second visit to Australia in 1964. The same year he went to Western Australia and set a water speed record of 276.33 mph. He was the only man to hold both water and land speed records and Australia had room for him to challenge both.

We drove to Geelong together, about 44 miles from Melbourne, in an E-type Jaguar. I was in the passenger seat. I can't tell you the top speed we travelled at, but it was a thrill, taking back roads and hugging the corners.

He was killed three years later at Coniston Water in Cumbria, U.K. His boat flipped over backwards travelling at over 300 mph. A song, "Out of this World," was written about the accident, as well as a film about Donald, "Across the Lake, " starring Anthony Hopkins as the great speed demon. I never saw the film: I was too sad over Donald's early death.

When I mention him to people today, I realize how old I am getting, as few have heard of him. So, look him up. Donald was a fabulous, fun man with incredible, but somewhat crazy, courage. **http://bit.ly/DonaldCampbell**

Other Purple Cow regulars were the stars of The Hathaways, a short lived television hit, especially in Australia in the early 60's. Human hosts chatted with three Marquis Chimps. Jack Weston was one of the stars and appeared in many movies in the years that followed. He was nominated for a Golden Globe Award as Best actor for a role in the 1976 movie "The Ritz." **http://bit.ly/TheHathaways**

The Hathaways stars were at the restaurant telling me wonderful stories about Elvis Presley, a next door neighbor to one of them. I was a big Elvis fan and fascinated by the humble shy Elvis they described. They talked about going to parties at Graceland where Elvis drank soft drinks, sat quiet and shy, changing the 45's on the record player. His bodyguards and guests, however, behaved a little wilder than that.

Of course, many local celebrities came to the restaurant too. The two I remember most were Olivia Newton John and Ian Turpie. Olivia Newton John starred in "Grease" with John Travolta in 1978. In 1982, she had a huge hit with the song *Let's Get Physical*. When she first came to the restaurant, she was 15. At that age, she was already a member of an all girls band *Sol Four* and was appearing in several daytime shows and weekly pop programs.

Bart Verhoff / Anefo Olivia Newton John in the pressroom, Schiphol-National Archive The Hague, 2.24.01.05 930-0132,license CC-BY-SA

Olivia's boyfriend at the time was Ian Turpie, a regular on a TV show called *Time for Terry*. They dined frequently at the *Purple Cow*. Ian was an Australian Entertainment legend. He covered almost everything in show business; acting, hosting, singing, you name it. He was incredibly successful and remained one of the most professional and well-liked celebrities. He died at a young age, at 68 in 2012, after being diagnosed with cancer a year before. At the time of his passing, he had been married to his wife Jan for 43 years. They had 3 children and 3 grandchildren.
http://bit.ly/IanTurpieIMBD

Olivia won a talent contest that earned her a trip to London and later to the United States.

Me? I stayed in Australia for another 22 years.

ASCO, Woolworths and Gillette

ASCO stood for Australian Services Canteens Organization and I worked as a manager of their canteens and clubs, traveling mainly around the states of Victoria and Tasmania, relieving managers going on holidays. I got to work on army, naval and air force bases.

It was during the Vietnam War. Canteens sold all you could possibly want, from toothpaste to clothing, a large array of cigarettes, dry cleaning services and a bar for drinks at the end of the day; mainly beer, it was Australia after all.

Then I worked as a Supermarket Manager with Woolworths. I was part of a new program to get managers quickly for all the new store openings. After a 6 month training course, I was given an address to go to. Arriving there, I found an empty paddock. I searched for and eventually found a phone booth and called my boss to get the "right" address.

I was told this was my new store; it will be ready in 6 months. It was my job to get it staffed and stocked and ready for the opening. This was great! But the store turned out to be way too small for the population explosion in that area. We could never fill the shelves fast enough and all worked long, long hours.

Woolworth's had decided to apply for liquor licenses in their stores to sell wine and spirits. Each manager had to have an individual license for that store. So I was sent to attend a 6 week course to learn all about wines and spirits. I loved the wine part a lot and owe my passion for fine food and wine to that experience.

When I returned to the store, it was even busier. We simply did not have enough space for the traffic we had. We had to do fill (restocking store shelves) during the opening hours, a real no-no in the industry then. A new supervisor came into the store and told me to "fix it or else".

After 16 hour days, 6 days a week, this was the wrong thing to say to me. I chose "else," gave him the keys to the store and told him, "you fix it," and left. While looking for another job following my outburst, I worked as a door-to-door salesman for awhile, selling cookware and encyclopedias; not fun!

Then I worked for a number of years with the Gillette® company. This company was **THE** Marketing Company in the world with one product hit after another. This job was the best marketing school you could have attended. I sold razor blades to pharmacies, and Papermate® and Flair® Pens to stationary and book stores.

Then I was promoted to be in charge of a newly formed personal care division that introduced hand held hairdryers and curling wands for consumers. This was the first time these small appliances would be sold for home use; a huge innovation at the time.

Then, women used bonnet hairdryers and men wore Brylcream®. Nobody styled at home; you went to a hairdresser or barber. Then came the "Dry Look," as Gillette described the new era. Men stopped using Brylcream® and women styled themselves with a hand held hairdryer. The products were called Supermax®, Max for Men®, Max Hatter® and Supercurl®.

Gillette® in Australia was one of the first places to launch these products, more or less a test marketing exercise. Senior management in Australia had little expectations for this category.

This new division had two employees; myself and a secretary. The product was made in Japan. TV ads hit the airwaves and all hell broke loose. We sold out in minutes all over the country. For the next twelve months most of the goods were being air freighted in from Japan. I would meet the jets coming in at midnight, arrange clearance through customs, and have trucks waiting with goods allocated to various retailers around the country. Again, I wasn't getting much sleep.

Retailers would call me night and day, promising to name their firstborn after me, begging or threatening for more goods to be allocated to them. Some tried bribes to get a larger share of the company's newest products.

By the end of the first year, this division was bigger in top line sales than the rest of the divisions put together. We were two people in that division, and there were over a thousand people involved around the country for all the rest of the products sold by Gillette®.

At the end of the twelve months I was promoted to State Manager, after achieving 30 times the forecasted sales. The person who took over from me had no chance to repeat these numbers as competitors started to enter this field quickly.

The biggest competitor became Braun®, a company Gillette® owned but had to operate separately due to Australia's concerns about a Gillette® monopoly. They dominated the Wet and Dry Shaver markets. So while results were consolidated, we were never allowed to talk to anyone at Braun®. Braun® stayed in this category, and after a few years and fading sales, the personal care division at Gillette® was closed.

On a trip to Brisbane, Queensland to see some customers, our flight was late and landed almost at midnight. I managed to grab the last cab. As we were taking off, a gentleman was running from the baggage area, also trying to get the last cab. I asked the driver to stop and see where the gentleman was going and possibly give him a ride.

As coincidence would have it, he was going to the same hotel. He hopped in the back with me and I reached out my hand and introduced myself. "My name is Roy Higgins," he said shaking my hand. Roy Higgins was the number one jockey in Australia; a national hero in a country that loves horse racing. He was named the greatest jockey ever in Melbourne, Australia. He won the Jockey Premiership 11 times and retired in 1983 with 2300 wins to his career. He won two Melbourne Cups; a race held the first Tuesday in November. The race is so important, there is a public holiday to honor the day. Over 100,000 people see the race live at the beautiful Flemington racetrack.

We exchanged contact information and the following year, I introduced Roy to Gillette® and he became a spokesman for them in a major Melbourne Cup promotion planned around him.

Roy was a gentleman through and through, and it was a thrill getting to know him. All this from giving a stranger a cab ride. Roy passed away at age 75 in 2014. There is a great book you may like to read about his life.
http://bit.ly/RoyHigginsJockey

Working for Gillette® was an amazing experience and my love of innovation and new products, well, let's just say I had great products to sell.

To give you an idea of what Gillette® and every manufacturer goes through to bring these innovative products to retail shelves, a lesson on the world of patents is one key to understanding this business. It is a simple world. There are only two types of patents, design and utility. The hard part is secrecy and speed; anyone can alter the idea and if the patent has not been granted, you and your idea have no protection against being copied.

A utility patent gives protection for twenty years over how the invention works; a new idea never done before. Say you make a car run on water instead of gas. That's a utility patent. Adding dimples on the George Foreman grill plates and adding "ski jumps" at the end of the plates, stopped the food from sliding off the surface while the fat drained at an angle. These two items became utility patents. If someone hears of your innovation and files the patent before you, there goes your idea.

A great patent lawyer will research quickly and let you know if your idea has been done before anywhere in the world. A great patent lawyer will also write the patent application in a way that blocks "derivatives", products that a competitor makes and adds a twist to in order to get around your patent. The stronger and tighter the utility patent is written, the stronger, and probably longer, your product will thrive in the marketplace.

The design patent is different from the utility patent. This patent lasts 14 years and is designed to protect how a product looks. A good design patent example is the Volkswagen Beetle. The car's shape is so distinctive that a similarly-shaped car would violate design patents and heavy fines would be leveraged against the fake "VW Beetle."

There were many innovations during my time at Gillette®. Earth Born® Shampoo using fruit as the natural fragrance promoting a PH balance that was right for hair, Right Guard® Deodorant for men, Flair® Pens using felt tips and ink, Papermate® Ball Point Pens with a life-time guarantee, GII® Shaver and Blades, SuperMax® line of personal care, Foamy® Shaving Cream… just to name the ones I can remember. Then, Gillette® Australia was always one of the top performing divisions in the world. Both the products and the management group there helped everyone be great.

My First Celebrity Product Endorsement with Gus Mercurio

Gus Mercurio 1974
Photo supplied by Russell Haig and Patrick Edgeworth

Leaving Gillette® was difficult for me, but an opportunity came along to be a Marketing Manager for Dunlopillo-Sleepmaker® in the mid 70's. The largest bedding manufacturer in Australia had factories in every major city, but fell to be number 3 in market share and was sinking further against competitors with successful marketing campaigns.

One was the Sealy® Posturepedic Bed. The other was Slumberland® who had more springs than anybody else and a great TV campaign showing a cement roller being driven over one side of the bed, while the other side of the bed had a person asleep undisturbed. Dunlopillo-Sleepmaker,® on the other hand, had a business model that focused on quick delivery of made to order beds with different ticking on the outside and made to order insides, not only in their brand but in many exclusive house brands too.

The first day on the job, I attended a sales meeting. During the meeting, we had a visitor, Gus Mercurio, who was the President of the Australian Chiropractic Association and a star of a hit TV series at the time called "Cash and Company."

Gus was born in Milwaukee, Wisconsin. While in the army, he was an amateur "Golden Gloves" fighter. When he left the army and became a professional boxer, his career was cut short by a punch to the throat that damaged his vocal chords. That punch also gave him back problems. The throat injury gave him a raspy voice and led to the hunt for a new career.

Getting his back fixed by a chiropractor motivated him to become a chiropractor. He moved to Australia, and had a successful practice that led to him being elected as president of the Australian Chiropractic Association. He became a referee for many boxing matches held in Melbourne, including several World Championship bouts.

The raspy voice bothered him. So, to strengthen it, he joined a local acting company and then was invited to be a commentator for boxing shows. He was soon discovered! This led to a very successful acting career in TV series and some character roles in movies seen around the world; Crocodile Dundee II and Blue Lagoon to name a couple. His son, Paul Mercurio, even took up acting and was the star of the hit movie *Strictly Ballroom*.

When I met Gus at this sales meeting he was already a star, but at the beginning of his acting career. But, I am getting ahead of myself; back to the sales meeting at Dunlopillo–Sleepmaker®. Gus addressed the sales meeting and told the salesmen how disappointed he was in licensing the Chiropractic® Bed endorsed by the Australian Chiropractic Association to Dunlopillo-Sleepmaker®. Sales were dismal, and the bed had less than 1% market share.

Motivated by Gus and his speech, I met Gus after the meeting and discussed with him about his being a personality to promote the bed on behalf of the Chiropractic Association. We made a deal.

Soon we had a marketing campaign ready. TV ads starring Gus and the Chiropractic® Bed went to air. He began making shopping centre appearances on center stage to educate shoppers about back care and how the Chiropractic Bed would solve or prevent back issues. This was the key to our success.

I would go on stage in the center of these major shopping centers and start introducing Gus. I would keep talking until enough of an audience stopped to look and listen. Then Gus would come out and do his thing. We travelled all over Australia when Gus's schedule allowed it. He was fabulous. We continued to improve on our shopping centre appearances and best of all, we had fun.

We added the "Perfect Spine" beauty contest to our repertoire, with the winners getting into the Miss Australia Pageant and raising funds for charities. We hired various TV actresses to appear with Gus so we had new material to go back to the places we had been before.

One of the actresses we travelled with for a while was Abigail. Abigail, a star in a steamy soap opera called "Number 96," was described as Australia's first sex symbol.

We were in a town in Northern Queensland one day, appearing in the one and only shopping center there. The center had to be closed, with security keeping anybody from getting in.

Dozens of doors were policed and it looked like we might have a riot. The whole town came out to see Abigail and Gus! It was an unbelievably huge success.

Dunlopillo-Sleepmaker® became number one with a market share as big as number 2 and 3 combined. In less than 2 years, we sold over 1 million Chiropractic® Beds. The population of Australia at that time was only 15 million.

Factories were working 24 hours a day and the lead-time to get a Chiropractic® Bed went from tomorrow to almost 6 months. Backorders kept growing no matter how much production increased. Eventually, the managing director called me in and gave me a set of golf clubs. He told me to stop promotions and take some time off to play golf so the company could catch up. After a few weeks I came back and went in to have a meeting with the Managing Director. I told him, "I'm not very good at golf and unlikely to ever be good at it, but I do have another idea."

The company was owned by Dunlop®, the people who knew about tires and rubber. The latex beds that we made at that time were too expensive for most of the population, but there was now technology for a high density foam that had most of the benefits of a latex mattress. Best of all, it was used by NASA for astronauts to sleep on in space. I told my boss that I could arrange for Apollo 11 to be brought to Australia and that Neil Armstrong would come and tour with the shuttle and promote a high density foam bed we already knew how to make.

The campaign was never approved. The company was satisfied where they were and did not know how they could manage if they had another hit on their hands.

Soon after, I left and became Managing Director of a Small Appliance Distributor called Goldair®. While the original Chiropractic Bed is still sold by Sleepmaker® and continues to be endorsed by the Chiropractic Association, Dunlopillo® focuses on latex beds with some other memory foam products.

Thirty years later, Tempur-Pedic® became a big hit in the USA, marketing High Density Foam Mattresses. I guess I was a little ahead of that coming trend.

Many, many years later, George Foreman and Gus would meet in Australia, while George was touring for the grill. This was no six degrees of separation: These men were two boxers who used what talents they had to make a success in other fields. It was a small world indeed and quite a wonderful feeling to see Gus and George together, boxing being the common denominator besides me. I put one man with a great bed and one man with a great grill and they both had huge success.

The "how to" did not change much in the 30 years between Gus's huge success as a spokesperson and George's huge success as a spokesperson.

Me? I just had more experience.

A few weeks before writing this chapter I received a wonderful Christmas card from Gus and his wife Rita. Gus died a few days after that.

Here is the news story with a moving statement from his son and information on his acting career.
http://bit.ly/GusMercurio82
http://bit.ly/GusMercurioIMBD

MY MENTOR: GÜNTER PETZ

I was hired by Goldex Trading Company as a National Sales and Marketing Manager. Two days after I started my new job, Gunter Petz of Nuremberg, Germany became the new owner of the company in Australia, when they failed to pay for merchandise supplied by him. Gunter was the sole shareholder of a company called EWT® (Elektro Warme Technic); it was the world's largest producer of fan heaters for all the major small appliance brands in the world.

He produced products for GE®, Phillips®, Bosch®, Siemens® and Allibert®, just to name a few. Goldex was also a customer he produced heaters for, but a customer that couldn't pay.

When he decided to take over, it became the first overseas company he owned. The heaters in Australia were sold under the brand *Goldair*®. He decided to move the company out of wholesale and into the retail market. The company changed its name from Goldex Trading to Goldair® and stopped being a wholesaler for other brands.

The challenge put before me was to develop our own brand Goldair® as fast as possible to replace the business we had dropped while representing other brands as a wholesaler.

We created a TV campaign featuring various toes in front of a new fan heater we had developed to launch. The product was shown in different rooms, with different toes in front of the heater, feeling warmth and comfort. The slogan for the TV commercial, and later for the entire product line we sold, was *10 out of 10 Mr. Goldair*®.

We went to air with almost zero distribution for the fan heater featured in the advertisement. Fortunately, the campaign created demand, we got distribution, and I kept my job. The heater was a huge success and the company entered into the market with other small appliances using the Goldair® name.

I was made Managing Director. The fan heaters, however, became such a major part of our business during the winter (June through August in Australia), the rest of the year we were searching for how to balance things out.

The first thing we did was start to sell LED watches, a new phenomenon in the market at that time. We took the EWT® name of our parent company and put it on the watches as a brand. It stood for **E**xciting **W**orld of **T**ime.

Watches were a Christmas business and we did well, but we still needed more sales in the summer to balance the growing winter fan heater business.

On the advice of our biggest customer, we took over a toy company in receivership.

We used the EWT name again. This time it stood for Exciting World of Toys. I loved this division. It was so much fun. Going to the toy show in New York, we looked at new products and decided what would sell in Australia. If you made a mistake in bringing in a toaster design, you could still close it out at a price to get your cost back.

A toy nobody wanted was a very costly closeout, so you could not afford many mistakes or you were out of business. This was a Christmas-only business and we were really lucky getting many memorable winners still on the shelves today. We launched Trivial Pursuit®, Rubik's Cube®, Transformers® and Cabbage Patch® Dolls.

These were all major hits. Cabbage Patch® Dolls, especially, were the hottest toy I remember, with lines outside stores for hours waiting for a shipment to arrive. Trivial Pursuit® almost caused a paper shortage in the world for all the printed cards used in the game. When Rubik's Cube® stopped selling at $10 a cube, it was closed out for 20c each. Fortunately, we had enough winners to absorb that loss.

We also had staple games and figures that were the foundation of our toy business; Shoots and Ladders®, Mousetrap®, and GI Joe® to name a few. These products sold steadily every year. GI Joe® sales always increased dramatically before the start of a war somewhere.

Günter was my mentor. He was a fabulous entrepreneur and businessman. He had invested in real estate from profits made selling fan heaters. Günter believed real estate would be there even if fan heaters became obsolete. He had some wisdom he used to share with me; sayings that guided me for the rest of my business career. Here are just a couple:

"Half drunk is a waste of money."

This saying was to teach me not to do anything halfway. If I believed in what I wanted to do, I was to go out and do it right. If I didn't do it right, I would fail. I used this quote many times myself to my managers over the years. It always got results. In a book by Donald Trump, *The Way to the Top,* there is a list of famous quotes by CEO's; he attributed that quote to me. But it was Gunter Petz who originated it. I just used it being a good student.

Another one of Gunter's sayings made me feel better at the end of many negotiations and deals:

"There is no bad deal doing business with people you like, and there is no good deal with people you don't like."

Gunter believed that sometimes in business, deals do not go as planned. But if you are around good people, that made up for a lot. If the person you were negotiating with was unpleasant or unlikeable, not making the deal was easier to bear. Gunter believed in the people he worked with.

Customers and their needs and desires were our stock and trade, and Gunter had seen every kind of relationship between buyer and seller under the sun. Here's another one of his sayings:

"Your best customer is the one whose file is the thinnest."

That summed up the experience, really. A salesperson needs to "get" the client and vice versa. When both sides of the equation, buyer and seller, are working with a thin, trouble-free file, that's when relationships in business are at their most successful, perhaps not always financially, but definitely satisfying.

"You can always get another customer, but losing a good supplier would be much more difficult to replace."

I always followed this piece of advice, which is why the supplier who developed the grill came to me first and not someone else. I always kept my word with our suppliers and was rewarded with many fabulous new products.

Gunter would also do something I loved. It became a part of his "brand." He'd be out with clients and customers and he'd meet new people in the bar. He would call the waiter over and say to him, "Bring me a bottle of Dom Perignon every 10 minutes until I say stop".

Everybody loved this, but I soon learned that Günter knew most restaurants and bars carry, at most, 12 bottles of Dom Perignon; usually, a lot less. So, an hour or so later, the waiter would be back saying they had run out. Groans ensued but Gunter was the man of the hour.

I thank you, Günter. Working with you was fun and memorable, a job I loved doing. Günter decided to sell the company one day. The new owners did not want the Toy division. So Gunter offered it to me. Negotiations did not go well. We parted company angry.

We got over it a couple of years later and continued to keep in touch now and then. Whenever we did meet in years to come, I enjoyed seeing him immensely.

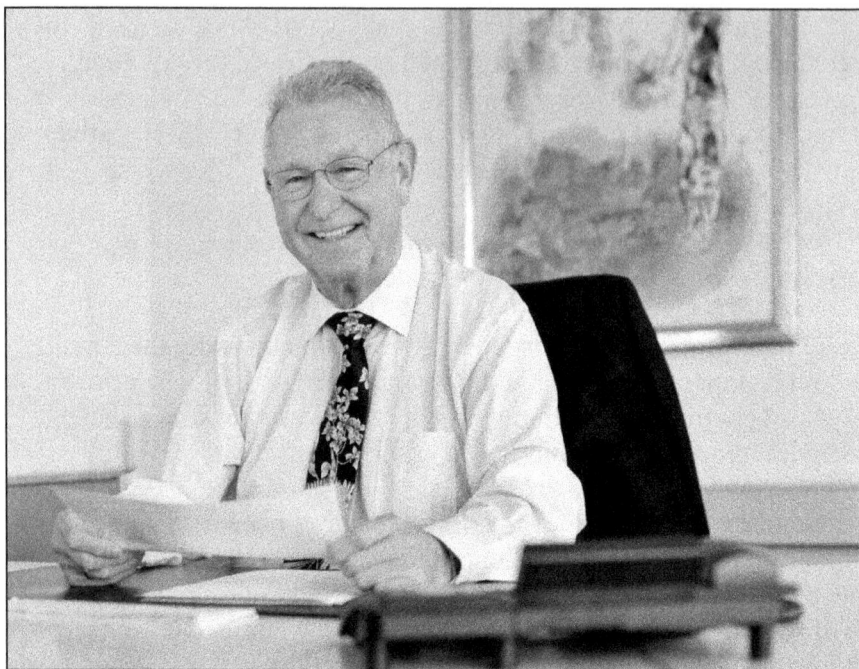

Günter Petz, Germany

I started my own company, Salton® Ltd., in Australia by licensing a brand known for Hotrays®. The brand was owned by Salton® UK who had the rights to the name all over the world, except for in the USA and Canada. Robin Klein was the Managing Director in the UK and his brother Martin stayed in South Africa and was involved with the Salton® brand there.

Robin eventually sold the company to Pifco® Ltd., who also owned the brand, Russell Hobbs®. The CFO from Goldair®, Milton Dickins joined the company and is one of my close friends to this day. One of our adventures was a product called, Fast and Fizzy®.

This device was invented in Sweden. Basically, you added water and a gas cylinder with a variety of flavors, then, you dispensed a carbonated soda drink in seconds. Fast and Fizzy® was to compete with a product called Soda Stream® from the UK that was a huge hit there and in Australia. Soda Stream® was dispensed into a bottle, and Fast and Fizzy® directly into a glass.

We had a big advantage, retailers loved it and gave us placement everywhere. However, Soda Stream® management had their own ideas of how to compete. They started out-spending us on television ads, 5 to 1. They hired people to go into stores where we were demonstrating the product and shout out "don't buy it, it might explode!"

One day, going home, I actually saw something under my car that looked like a bomb. After the police were called and it was deemed a harmless "fake" bomb, I received an anonymous phone call. A voice told me if I did not stop selling Fast and Fizzy®, next time there would be a real bomb under my car. It was funny and scary at the same time.

Soda Stream® was spending so much money to fight us; I got worried. I had a lot of inventory arriving and on order and would soon be out of money fighting a rather unorthodox competitor.

I was pushed into a corner, so I went to one of my favorite merchandise managers who was with Woolworths® at the time. Fast and Fizzy® and Soda Stream® were retailing for about $70. I offered to sell Woolworths 100,000 Fast and Fizzy® Machines for 1c each. All they had to do was buy 12 bottles of syrup and a spare gas cylinder for each machine they purchased at this price so they could service the customer who bought the machine.

He jumped at the deal. I was able to absorb the loss of giving away the machine from the gross margins of selling the flavor syrups and the extra CO_2 cylinder. The deal made it possible to pay off the loan the bank gave me to bring the machines to Australia and put the 'drinks war' to an end overnight.

Woolworths® ran the ad for the machine on the cover of their weekly magazine. They sold the machines at $9.95 and sold out 5 minutes after the doors opened. They did make a mistake however, by not making the consumer buy the syrup at the same time. Consumers could buy any syrup anywhere and perhaps for less; all the flavors worked the same.

Woolworths took a year to get rid of the syrups. Soda Stream®
soon went almost bankrupt and was sold. It changed hands a few
times and was re-launched using a healthier drinks angle in 1998.
Soda Stream® seems to be the only brand selling a home
carbonating machine and doing well to this day, though Cuisinart®
is making a run for it.

Fast and Fizzy® disappeared out of the market everywhere that I
tried to find it. So, while these tactics in business are not my cup of
tea, it worked for Soda Stream® to get rid of a competitor. However,
I am not sure it was worth the cost.

At the time of writing this, many years later, new owners of Soda
Stream® took Soda Stream® public in the USA. The product is
doing well with an excellent "recycling" marketing angle.

When I arrived in the USA in 1987, I remember a similar drinks
war story. This one was about beer.

Corona® was ranked number two among imported beers in the
U.S.A, gaining on the leader Heineken®. You walked into a bar and
saw a bottle of Corona® with a lime in the neck along with many
beer drinkers.

Somehow a story spread that during manufacturing, Corona® had
Mexicans urinate into the beer. Sales plummeted. Then a Heineken®
distributor was sued and had to issue a public apology on the news
and stated that some of their over ambitious salesmen told the story
as a bad joke. There was no truth to it and they were sorry. Well, for
all the people that had not heard the rumor, they heard it then and
Corona sales plummeted even more. Heineken® remained the top
imported beer.

In 2009 however, reports put Corona® Extra back on top as the
number one imported beer in the USA.

All these experiences were put to good use. I remembered the
lessons about successful launches of innovative products and how to
maintain longevity for products in the marketplace.

MEETING MY NEW PARTNERS:
DAVID SABIN AND BILL RUE

Attending the International Chicago Housewares Show for the first time in 1986, I met David Sabin, CEO of a group called SEVKO, which owned the US division of Salton® Inc. David and I instantly clicked. He offered me a job as President of this division and asked me to move from Australia to the USA and help him build this division from $8 million in sales to $50 million.

He thought this could be done with some acquisitions pretty quickly.

I sold Salton® Australia and moved to Chicago on April 1st, 1987.

In the first few months in the United States, I tried and failed at getting an acquisition to create a division that could generate sales of $50 million. During these efforts, I got to know Bill Rue, CFO of SEVKO. David and Bill were always available when I had questions and needed advice.

David's partners in SEVKO had little patience with the Salton division and decided to sell it, or close it down ASAP. David felt bad I had come all the way from Australia and did not get a chance to build Salton®.

David helped me raise funds to do a LBO (leveraged buyout) for the Salton® division. Mesirow Venture Capital became our partner in this LBO.

Thus, David Sabin, CEO of SEVKO, and Bill Rue, CFO of SEVCO, would join this new partnership, creating a new company in America based on the drive of an Australian. That's my kind of globalism.

Bill and I hired 5 employees and moved to new offices to start Salton®. Our Sales were about $8 million. We only had a few products: *The Wet Tunes*® shower radio, *The Three for All*® coffee and espresso maker combination, *Hotrays*® and *Split Decision*®, a dual carafe coffeemaker. The company was small, but it had a reputation for innovation from the beginning when Lou Salton founded it in 1947. After a few months, David left SEVKO and joined me and Bill at Salton®.

The Three Musketeers were on the way.

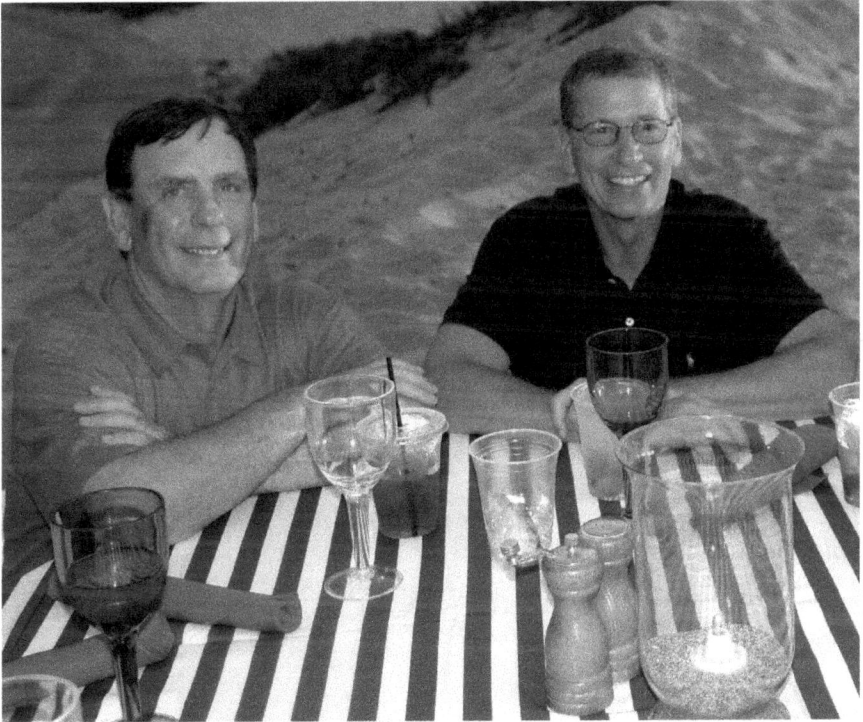

Bill Rue and David Sabin in 2007

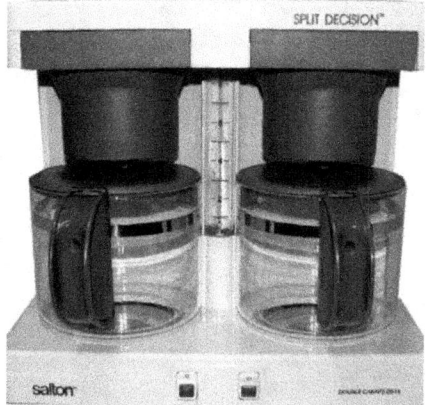

The Salton® Hotray®, Wet Tunes®, The Three for All® and Split Decision®

INFOMERCIAL INNOVATION

Our first big break at Salton® came when a customer in Florida told me they had seen an infomercial for a sandwich maker.

While this product had been around for years, no one knew how versatile it was until the infomercial aired. Burdines®, a Department Store Chain in Florida that was part of the Federated Group (now Macy's®), could not get inventory anywhere now that this TV infomercial was creating demand. They were constantly sold out.

Sandwich-makers were a staple in Australia (think YEARS before the American panini maker craze.) I knew a supplier who made a patented scissor action sandwich maker that not only cooked, but cut and sealed the sandwich when the lid was closed. I contacted Chiaphua's corporate owner, Herbert Chang, in Hong Kong. We soon had a huge shipping container of sandwich makers on the way to Burdines®. We rode the coat tails of the on air advertising and soon were shipping over 100,000 units a month to retail customers. Salton sold a good quality product that consumers raved about. It didn't matter that it wasn't the identical unit that was on television. Consumer satisfaction was always the sweet spot we searched for; it went hand in hand with profit.

The infomercial first launched in Florida by a retired businessman who did an amazing job selling the product in the video. Soon there were two sandwich maker infomercials on air nationally. Both retailing for $49.95. One was the Clark Snakmaster by Clark National Products based out of California and the other was the SuperSnacker from a company based out of New York. Research has indicated that the SuperSnacker sold more than $35 million dollars worth of product on air. It is also worth noting that it starred a celebrity, Christopher Hewitt, who was best known for his character on the sitcom Mr. Belvedere. They must have seen the potential in having a celebrity spokesperson to pitch a product on national television and it worked.

We had started with $68,000 of capital. Our sales went to $50 million as the infomercials aired. At that time, we were turning over our capital twice a day. While this was a big success, it was the most stressful time I have ever felt in business.

Meeting payroll was a constant challenge. Cash was needed to pay for the appliances and finance receivables or the shipments would stop. Retailers would have become irate and/or disappeared. To raise money, we took the company public. We were listed on the NASDAQ stock exchange under the symbol SALT for $12 a share.

The sandwich maker had been around for decades so anybody could make and sell it. Competitors jumped into this field quickly. Soon pricing dropped from a $50 retail price point down to $10 for a poorly made product. Inferior quality soon killed consumer and retail interest.

We were left with orders to our suppliers but no orders from customers in the USA. We fulfilled our commitments by converting our orders to suppliers for a variety of different waffle makers and pizzelle makers. These products used the same components and our commitment to our suppliers was honored. Our shares after going public, however, dropped to below $1.

1990s Sandwich Maker

Another infomercial making big waves was the *Juiceman®* Juice Extractor. The video featured bushy eyed Jay Kordich as its salesman. Soon we were selling juice extractors with everybody else. TV sales stopped for the *Juiceman®* Company when similar, inferior products were introduced at lower pricing and quality in retail stores; a repeat of the Sandwich Maker story.

Trillium, the *Juiceman®* company did some retail business, but in a very modest way. They were concerned their TV business would be killed if the product was sold readily in all stores. My group had learned from its sandwich maker experience that when inferior products entered and flooded the market, it was time to change course.

We approached Trillium to acquire it, with all its patents, brand and infomercials. Our board, who at that time included Jim Tyree and Tom Galuhn from Mesirow and Victor Barnett from Financo, approved the deal quickly. Victor Barnett, the Chairman of Burberry's, especially saw the potential of doing television to drive retail sales for the same product.

Juiceman® sales were down to $4 million. Rick Cesari, director and part owner of Trillium, continued helping us make new *Juiceman®* infomercials and to buy media effectively. Steve Cesari, Rick's brother, and Robert Lamson, also part owners of Trillium, stayed in touch with the company and helped to make this acquisition a success for Salton®. *Juiceman®* was soon doing $50 million of very profitable sales. The company fortunes started to rise rapidly. Various successes quickly followed, and now we had a new formula.

Here is a link to a clip showing Jim Carey playing the Juiceman in a skit. Hilarious. A must see. I believe imitation is the greatest form of flattery. We showed this to everybody.
http://bit.ly/JuiceWeasel

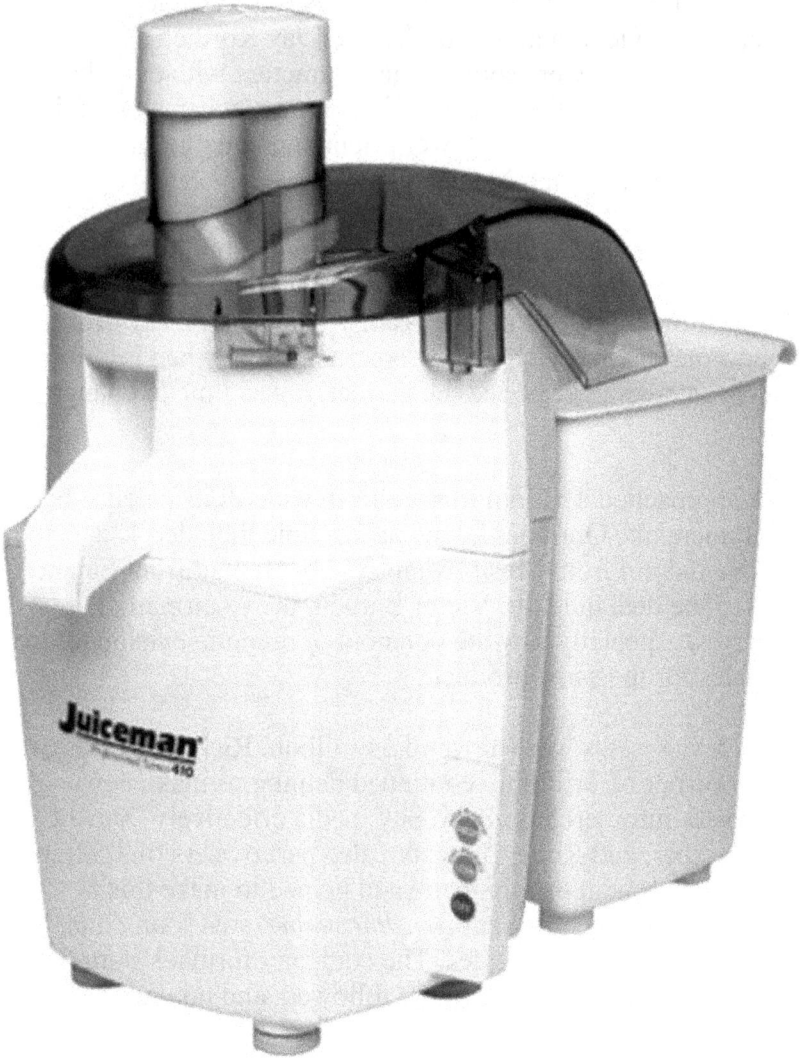

Juiceman® Juice Extractor

Breadman® was another product with an infomercial ready to launch by the Trillium Company. We got the rights to it when we bought the company. We aired the bread maker infomercials and took the product to retailers. The bread machine category grew rapidly and *Breadman®* remained the brand to buy and was the market leader, years after most competitors stopped selling in this category.

The bread makers we sold had revolutionary features. We kept adding new innovations and in my humble opinion, were far ahead of all the competition. Julia Child used to come and see us at trade shows. She loved our products and was a popular television chef and cook book author for many decades. Julia inspired the movie, Julie and Julia released in 2009 starring Meryl Streep and Amy Adams.
http://bit.ly/JuliaChildBIO

Julia also gave us wonderful tips on how to improve our appliances for the home cook. We listened, and with our suppliers and in-house engineers, created some enhancements based on her advice and were able to patent a number of innovations she inspired.

For instance, we added an automatic Fruit and Nut Dispenser so that at just the right time in the mixing and baking cycle, fruit and nuts would drop into the dough to make sweet breads in the Breadman®. We also developed a bread machine with a bagel feature and removable bagel trays and programming to bake a seven-grain bread, which other machines were not strong enough to do.

We had other great TV products to take to retailers too. A partnership was formed with Ron Popeil. Some folks may remember his late night commercials and his company Ronco's inventions. (Chop-o-matic, Mr. Microphone and the Smokeless Ashtray were a few of his better-known products.) He would sell products on TV with Infomercials and we would distribute his products to retail stores. The first product we started selling was a huge hit; a Ron Popeil Pasta Maker.

Ron Popeil and the Pasta Machine
Photo courtesy of HomeWorld Business/ICD Publications

Salton® kept increasing its product range and capabilities. By 1996, we had acquired the White Westinghouse® small appliance license royalty agreement and an exclusive contract to sell the goods to Kmart®. Our sales were nearing $300 million, and we were the most talked about company in the industry.

Later, with the success George Foreman added to the mix, we launched *Rejuvenique®* with Linda Evans. *Rejuvenique®* was brought to us by a group of physicians who developed a mask with a battery operated electric current in strategic places that stimulated muscles in the face and reduced wrinkles as a result.

Sam Perlmutter, an attorney, who had introduced us to George, introduced us to Linda Evans. We also sold some skin care products with this mask. Linda Evans, before agreeing to be in the infomercial, did her own testing with the product and did not accept our clinical trials as satisfactory proof. She wanted to see results for herself.

Linda went to a beauty salon where she was a customer in Seattle, and got a group of women to volunteer to use the mask for 30 days. I repeat, these women were not paid.

All came back raving about the product and the benefits they saw. Our infomercial with Linda Evans included many of these women from Linda's test. They appeared in the infomercial without pay.

Linda Evans is the definition of the word "Lady". What a wonderful, genuine and beautiful person. We all loved her at Salton®. The product did well quickly with sales close to $50 million.

Soon after, however, the company got a letter from the FDA telling us the claims we made were not acceptable. We would be fined thousands of dollars if we continued selling the product. This letter also went to all of our customers. The product was dead overnight. We fought the FDA with lawyers and documentation but it was Linda Evans who went with me to Washington to meet with an Illinois Senator. That got us the breakthrough we needed. He got us an interview with the FDA to present our case.

Leon Dreimann and Linda Evans
Photo courtesy of HomeWorld Business/ICD Publications

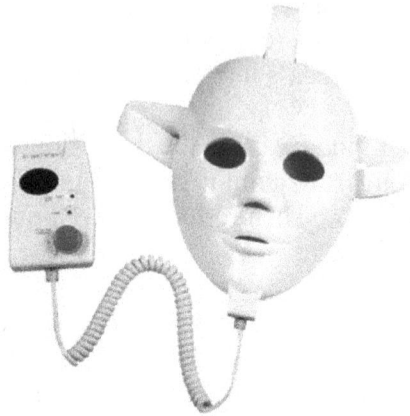

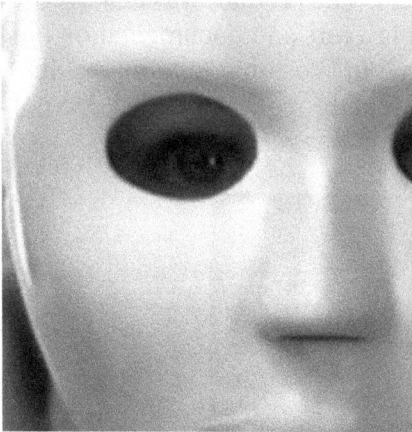

Rejuvenique®

The FDA, after seeing our clinical trials and results, agreed we did not make claims that could not be substantiated. They retracted the letter warning us not to sell and gave us a new letter telling us we could resume selling with the parameters they set for the claims we could make.

However, over a year went by before we received the letter that would allow us to continue sales. No retailer was willing to go back to selling Rejuvenique, and I had to regrettably discontinue this product. My wife loved the skin care. When she ran out, she was very disappointed. Recently, my daughter Samantha found more online and got it for her as a birthday present. Her step-mother was very happy with this gift.

During this period, we also launched a product called *Thunder Mixer*® with Hulk Hogan. This hand held, battery operated blender, sold a few hundred thousand units before many product copies flooded the market and we had to drop the item. My daughters, Alana and Michelle, use it today to make protein shakes. They guard the samples we have left and are very concerned about how they would replace the Thunder Mixers we have left in the house when the last one finally breaks down.

No, we never considered using Hulk Hogan for the grill. We liked working with Hogan, who in the time we spent with him, was a gentleman, very talented and likeable. By the time we talked to Hogan's agent about the Thunder Mixer®, our deal with George was already well on the way. Hulk did come out with his own grill, you can see it on line.

Not everything we did was a hit. I have to tell you about our biggest flop. A star of a daytime soap opera and his beautiful wife came to us with an invention they wanted to develop and sell as an infomercial. They were willing to be in the infomercial to give this product an extra chance.

The product was called "Flush'n'Shut." It was a device you attached to the toilet flush lever and the toilet seat. When you flushed, if the seat was up, it would automatically come down. It was easy to install and had a retail of $20 for two of them. We agreed with the inventor it was a great idea. No more arguments with your wife about not putting the seat down. Dogs would not be able to drink from the toilet bowl. Curious toddlers would be safe from easy germ access.

We went to air with a short form infomercial. One of the major costs involved with making a sale, besides airtime for infomercials, was the call center that takes the orders. So, after our first couple of weeks of testing the show on TV, we got a huge bill from the call center, but very few orders in proportion to the calls we received; about twenty calls to one order. So, the call center expense alone was higher than the retail revenue coming in. We could not understand the problem.

As it turned out, most of the calls were from kids wanting to tell toilet jokes. Unfortunately, this great idea was flushed away.

Another great product we did was a trick bike with 3 wheels, called WRFF® or Walk Run Fly Faster. We went to air with a commercial starring Snoop Dogg. We had a great advert with great lyrics written by, of course, Snoop Dogg. The product was sold exclusively at Toys R Us® at a retail of $299. A well-made quality product and beautifully designed, it was capable of great tricks that could be performed safely.

WRFF was available in a variety of colors and there was a limited edition Snoop Dog version pimped out with spinning rims, a tribal paint design, tassels and flashing lights.

The WRFF did not sell fast enough for Toys R Us® and after too short a time, they reduced the price to $99 without talking to us and cancelled all their orders that were on the way to them from overseas. At $99, it sold out quickly. They wanted more at that price. We could not make a quality product to retail at $99, so this great product was discontinued and ruined by a retailer with no patience.

WRFF

THE PRODUCT OF PRODUCTS

In 1993, one of our suppliers came to see us at our offices in Illinois, USA. The supplier was Tsann Kuen, a Taiwanese company, with manufacturing facilities in Xiamen, China. Mr. TK Wu was Chairman and the major shareholder of this publicly traded company. Mr. Wu was a charming man with a wonderful enthusiasm for new products, innovation, and design. He was one of the best entrepreneurs I had the pleasure to know, not only in China, but anywhere in the world.

He brought a team with him to our offices to show us a variety of new products Tsann Kuen had developed. TK was always enthusiastic and professional in his presentations. He had a sales manager discuss the commercial aspect, an engineer present the technical and manufacturing options. A designer/engineer team who were based in United States, but did projects for Tsann Kuen also attended this meeting. One of the products was a small grill.

Michael Boehm and Robert Johnson presented the product features and their ideas about why it would succeed in the USA. It grilled both sides of food at the same time and was basically the same concept as a sandwich maker. The twist, however, was the idea that it would be ideal for making tacos. The design reminded you of tacos, it came with a forked spatula that fit in the grooves of the grill and would be used to scrape food into a taco held on a plastic tray under the edge of the grill.

Our team liked the idea but felt a taco maker was too one dimensional. Because it was so small we thought it would be great for a single person to grill a great burger, a steak, a piece of salmon or a chicken breast. I suggested the product needed to be at a much greater angle to make the food easier to be removed.

The factory said this would not work as the fat would drain during cooking into the taco shell before the food was scraped into it. Our team thought this was even better. Healthy cooking, drain the fat and grill the food without it sitting in fat.

Since the product was basically finished we had to be creative in incorporating these ideas. An extra set of back legs was proposed by the engineers, to be attached to the back legs of the grill, creating a forward angle. We agreed on two drip trays one placed in front of the grill to catch unwanted fat as it sizzled off and ran downhill. This tray was used at the same time as grilling burgers, steaks, chicken etc together with the leg extenders to create the angle. The second tray would be used without the leg extenders and would hold a taco and food grilled would be "taco fillings".

The idea appealed to me but I told the factory, the design seemed too small for the USA. They may want to do something bigger with the same idea. However, in the meantime, a gourmet show was coming up in San Francisco where we exhibited each year. I would be happy to present the little downhill grill to our customers, get a reaction and possibly sell some. (We always believed in under-promising and over-delivering with our suppliers).

We discussed various names for the product. Being a movie buff, my suggestion "Lean, Mean, Fat Reducing Grilling Machine" won the day. The movie I had in mind was *The Longest Yard* with Burt Reynolds. He played a quarterback for a prison team called the "Mean Machine," who had to play against a prison guards' team.

You will read later how and why this model was closed out for 1c each and the evolution of this product later in the book.

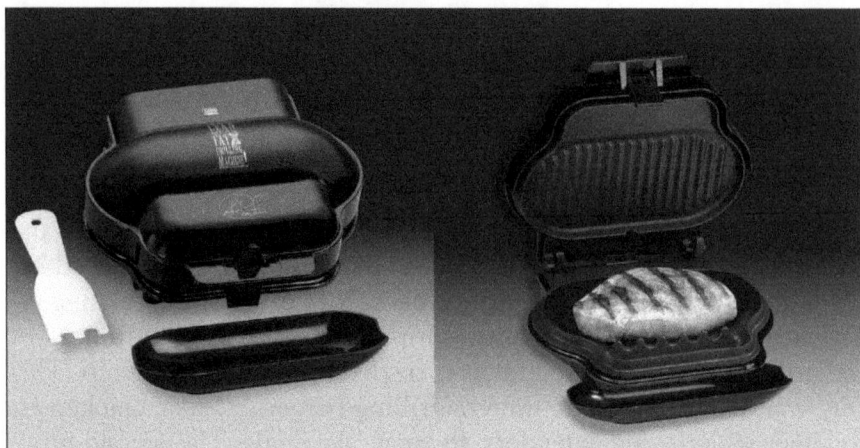

Original Grill Design Model # GR8

Burt Reynolds in The Longest Yard 1974

The product was ready to sell. In our testing, we found it worked really well, but everyone kept saying "it's small." The grill only had room to cook two burger patties or one chicken breast at a time.

In April that year at the Gourmet Show, our customers were not interested in the concept of this grill. The main reason was our launch to retailers of the Ron Popeil Pasta Machine. Ron was at the show demonstrating the machine, making pasta for everybody, and the retailers loved it.

Ron had already successfully launched the product on TV with an infomercial, so retailers were excited to sell it in their stores. At the end of the four day show, a friend, Michael Srednick, a veteran in the industry, asked to talk to me.

Michael was responsible for putting the deal together between Salton and Popeil. Michael asked me if he could sell the grill to a potential customer he had.

I was rather surprised. Michael already had someone interested and I told him our success was zero. No one had shown interest after 4 days of presenting the product. I told him he was welcome to sell the product to whoever he wanted to, but he would need to make all the arrangements with the factory himself.

We would not introduce it to the market ourselves. I gave Michael our contact at Tsann Kuen and informed them we would not be going ahead with the grill. They could sell it to Michael Srednick directly.

Michael never told me who the customer was and I did not ask. Almost a year later, I was sitting in my office reading my mail when I received a phone call from him. He told me he was calling about the grill. He wanted to tell me who his customer was. I was listening, but continued reading my mail at the same time.

Michael told me about a dinner a friend of his, a Los Angeles attorney by the name of Sam Perlmutter, attended over a year ago. The guest of honor at this dinner was George Foreman.

During dinner, many of the people made product suggestions for George to endorse. George did not respond to any of the ideas. However, he told the group that what he really would like to sell was a grill that made a great juicy burger.

Everybody knew how George Foreman loved a good hamburger. Sam took note of this idea and told his friend Mike. Mike saw the grill at the Salton Booth in San Francisco and thought this was exactly what George was suggesting.

When I gave the grill deal to Mike and Sam, he sent a sample to George to try. After many months, George's wife Mary saw the sample, tried it and really liked it. She cooked meals on it for George and told him he should sell this product as it grilled really well.

George contacted Mike and Sam through his attorney at the time, Henry Holmes, and told them he was willing to endorse the product, but wanted a great marketing company to do it.

"So," says Michael "that's the story. Will you be the company to market this grill with George Foreman's endorsement?" I laughed and said "Michael, I already got rid of this product. Now you want me to take it back? How will it help to have a boxer sell a food product? I don't see how it would do any better being reintroduced than it did the first time around."

As I said this, I saw a letter saying the Gourmet Show was being moved to Las Vegas this year because construction was running late at the Moscone Center in San Francisco.

An idea started forming in my head. George Foreman …Vegas… Gourmet Show…PR… Cocktail party with our major customers to meet George Foreman in Vegas. This could be fun and great for Salton!

So, I tell Mike, we will do it. We wanted George to come to Vegas to introduce the product, meet our customers at a cocktail party, and be at our booth to sign autographs and help with the product demonstrations. We would not pay any appearance fees or any royalties. We would be George's partner.

Salton would take all the expenses out first, including SGA (Selling and General Administration expenses). Then we would split profits on a 50/50 basis. The following week we signed the contract. Sam and Mike, who put this deal together, would get 7.5% each, George 45% and Salton 40%.

Our marketing team kept the original name. Barbara Westfield, our Marketing Manager at that time, became the product manager for this item. She added George Foreman's signature to the top of the product and created a slogan for the packaging; "Knock Out The Fat."

We prepared samples, mocked up packaging and had Keith Hamden, our head of sales, and David Sabin, our Chairman, call all our key customers who would be attending the show in Vegas. They invited our buyers to a pre-dinner cocktail party for a meet and greet with George Foreman. About 75 people accepted our invitation.

Vegas, here we come.

George with Sam Perlmutter

VEGAS

Ron Popeil was a director at the Mirage Hotel, so that is where we stayed. My assistant, Juanita Rusin, who was loved by all who met her, was indispensible to me and missed dearly in my retirement, was given the responsibility to take care of George. Her instructions were to get him a suite, meet him when he arrived, take him to the "meet and greet" and then to our booth the next day to sign autographs and demonstrate the grill.

Make sure he has all he needs, I told her. Sounded simple enough, but the simpler it seems, the harder it usually is. My daughter Samantha who was a Product Manager for Salton at the time, was there to help.

Shortly before George arrived, the hotel informed Juanita the suite wasn't ready. A frequent customer who gambled at the Mirage had not yet checked out, so Juanita was to come back in a few hours. No matter what we said, the message was clear; gamblers come first. George can wait. Only a pit boss could make an exception. So, Juanita asked a pit boss to release the suite to George. Come back this afternoon was the answer.

Juanita called me and told me she needed my suite to have George rest and wait for his suite to become available. My wife and I left our suite, met her in the lobby with our key, just as George arrived, wearing dark glasses and looking pretty good.

A week earlier, George defended his World Championship belt against Axel Schultz. George won but still had a black eye healing from the fight. So the dark glasses stayed on.

The first thing I noticed was how people reacted to George. As soon as they recognized him, they rushed to get a closer look. George responded with hellos and there was a wonderful smile on his face that was very infectious. People who got close to him began smiling immediately too.

We saw that the longer he stayed in the lobby, the more the crowds grew. Juanita grabbed him and took him to a nearby restaurant in the hotel away from the gathering crowds to have a quick lunch and meet with me. She raced up to the suite to make sure it was all clear and ready for George to rest and wait for his suite to be ready.

Finally, I got to meet George. My hand almost disappeared in George's hand at our first handshake. He had a gentle grip and a wonderful peaceful charisma about him. I told him who would be at the cocktail party that evening and what to expect the following day at the show.

Juanita took George to the suite; then, she called me to say she needed to find some security for George when he walked around the hotel, at the party and to the booth the following day. It was suggested we have security around all the time, but at a discreet distance. I was surprised this was necessary. George would be meeting major retail executives who met celebrities all the time and were not easily impressed. I agreed it might be a useful precaution, and we did want George to be happy with all the arrangements.

I thought the meet and greet that night would last 1 to 2 hours at the most. We bought tickets to hand out to our customers for the *Siegfried and Roy Show* at the Mirage and *Mystere* at Treasure Island next door.

George moved into his suite later in the afternoon and was picked up by Juanita and a couple of security people from the hotel just before 6pm. When I saw him arrive at our private room where guests were arriving, I saw why he needed security. He was like a Pied Piper with a long line of people following him through the casino.

Once he was in our private party room, George would be safe, I thought. Wrong again. All of our customers and our own people surrounded him as soon as he entered. I started to get an inkling that we may have found ourselves a pretty good partner. We managed to get a few tables setup and put George behind them. A line was forming for people to come and meet George, get an autograph, and take a photo with him.

Everybody in the room loved being with George, and he was tireless. He talked with everybody, told great stories, and was generous taking photos, despite the black eye. He signed autographs and best of all, he didn't look at the time. I, however, was looking at the time. We had almost 100 tickets for the early and late shows and nobody wanted them. They wanted to stay and hang out with George.

Juanita had the idea to go and hand out the tickets outside of the theatres to families and couples who were waiting in the ticket purchase line (just in case none of our guests showed up.) We made some people pretty happy from what I heard.

The "meet and greet" lasted 3 ½ hours. I put a halt to it finally and had Juanita take George back up to his suite. This gave us the opportunity to have some people go and use the tickets we had for the late show times.

I retired for the night excited about the next day. We had an early start to introduce the world to the "The Lean Mean Fat Reducing Grilling Machine" demonstrated by George Foreman.

The organizers of the Gourmet Show knew we were bringing George in the morning and assigned some security to help get George into our booth. He was to stay as long as we needed him and help demonstrate the grill. Ten minutes after his arrival, it was pandemonium.

People converged on our booth from every corner of the showroom floor. Aisles were blocked as far as you could see. We could not move anywhere, and security immediately called for backup. They cleared a space for George and led him to an area upstairs, close to our booth, with glass windows overlooking the hall. We were told George could not go back to our booth as no one was prepared to handle the crowds in this space.

So the demos went on without George. The crowds left. Barbara Westfield, our Marketing Manager, took a photographer upstairs to get some photos of George for our packaging, instruction manuals, and recipe books. George was tireless and gave us all we needed. The design of the packaging that she and George began that day was used around the world for many years to come.

Some press came and we took them upstairs to get interviews. I remember one magic moment when I got to see what George was really like. George was looking out from the upstairs window and noticed a lady standing outside our booth with a pen and photo, looking very sad that she had missed him. It looked like she had been waiting for quite some time.

George asked us to go and see the lady and bring her upstairs. He did not want her to go away disappointed. She wanted the autograph as a gift for her husband for his birthday; he was a big fan. When she left, her face told me she would now be an even bigger fan of George Foreman than her husband. That was the moment, I thought to myself, 'I would make this work no matter what it takes.'

The next day, George went back to Houston. That morning, I read a *USA Today* interview with George from the day before. He was quoted as saying, "I will make a million dollars from this grill." When I said goodbye to him, I mentioned the quote. I told him $1,000,000 is a lot of zeros. It would be pretty tough to get to this target, but we would do our best!

Later that day, Ron Popeil walked up to me and suggested that we do an infomercial for the grill with him and George, together. I was almost speechless. Ron never worked in an infomercial with anybody, nor did he ever do a product he did not develop himself. This was big. Nobody had been more successful than Ron Popeil on TV.

I immediately said "yes" and asked, "how soon could we do this?" Ron said to me, "not so fast". The grill was too small. Once I had a larger one, then we would talk again.

THE INFOMERCIAL

I contacted Rick Cesari, the producer of the Juiceman® and Breadman® infomercials. We continued working together after he and his partners sold us Trillium. I told him all about George and the product as well as Ron Popeil's interest.

Rick started chomping at the bit. We both agreed this could be big. We formed a strategy. We would sell the small grill to retailers and launch the larger grill in an infomercial, holding it back in the beginning from retail for a few months.

We took some orders from department stores and specialty retailers for the small grill, and it was on the shelves within a couple of months after the Vegas launch. Macy's was the first to place an order and many others followed soon after.

The factory had a larger design ready based on our first meeting over a year before and the comments I made then. We approved the same design and started tooling for it immediately. Some weeks later, I took a larger grill, almost twice the size of the original grill, to Ron and said, "Ok here it is, let's go".

Ron looked at it and said it was still too small. He wanted one double the larger size I'd just handed him. I contacted the factory, and again, they started working on an even bigger grill.

In the meantime, I said to Rick that we couldn't wait for Ron any longer. Let's do an infomercial with George for the larger grill we have now and when the Super Size is ready, we can go back to Ron then. We had promised our customers and George there would be a TV infomercial, so we needed to shoot it now.

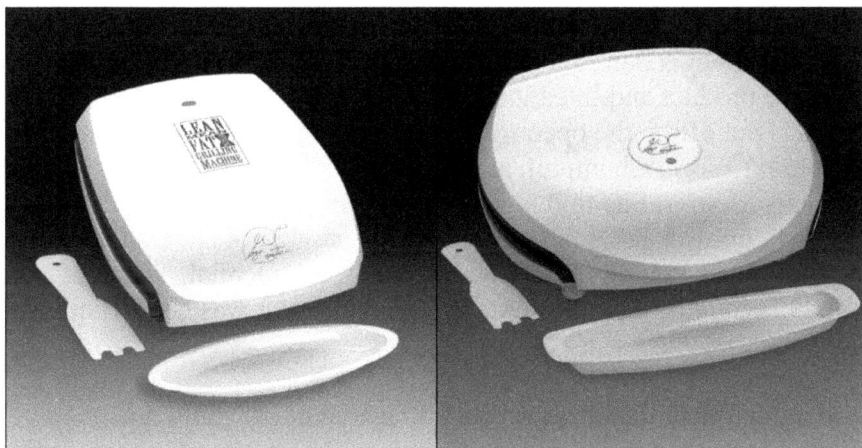

Left: GR20 Family Size. Right: GR30 Jumbo Size

We shot the infomercial and put it on air a couple of months later. We liked the look of it. George was fabulous. It failed! Not what people want to remember! Some thought it was an instant hit. So, we tweaked it and tweaked it. We dropped the retail from $89.95 to $59.95, but still, it was no good.

In the meantime, retailers were getting antsy. Their inventory of the small grill was not moving and many started to lose patience with the product. My Board was beginning to ask questions of how much more money we would blow on this idea. The only one not losing patience was George. He kept being positive and available, despite not seeing any checks.

Some retailers were demanding to return their inventory. I was running out of time. Almost 18 months had passed but I was stubborn. I could feel we were close, if only I could find the right twist. Consumers who had bought the product and wrote us letters were telling us how much they liked it. Rarely does this happen. Usually, consumers only write to complain. Praise was very rare indeed. All signs were that we had something ready to explode in the marketplace.

Then one day, one of my customers and friend, Mike Krauter, from the Macy's San Francisco store, called me. He said his wife used the product and liked it a lot. She also watched the infomercial, but was put off by the opening scene showing George Foreman becoming World Champion at the age of 45 by knocking out Michael Moorer. She told him she liked George talking and demoing the grill, but was not a fan of boxing. She could not understand why we would use boxing footage in a cooking infomercial. This was only 30 seconds of a 30-minute infomercial, so it was not difficult to take out.

I agreed with this observation 100 per cent and could not understand how we all missed this point. The next week a crew went to Houston, Texas, and shot footage of George and his sons in the kitchen of their home.

As soon as this aired, we were a hit. We were better than break even, with numbers improving every day. Red ink stopped. Black ink started. Our airtime started to increase daily, and the results kept getting better and better.

We released the grill that was on TV to retailers and told them it was a hit, but no one believed us. They did not want the larger grill and still insisted on returning the small one.

We needed something out of the box, a huge incentive for them to support us with retail distribution of the larger grill. So, we offered our retail customers the small grill, including what they had in inventory for 1 cent. They could sell the original small grill for whatever price they wanted, as long as they bought the larger grill and let us create the demand for them.

That appealed to nearly all of them and we got the distribution we wanted. A couple of the retailers said no; this must be some trick and they would not fall for it. I could only laugh at this idiocy. Interestingly, these few retailers that said no are not in business as retailers today.

The jumbo size grill was now ready, and we did another infomercial for it. We did not go back with the jumbo size to Ron Popeil. The George Foreman Grill was taking off and we decided to go without Ron. But he was right, the bigger the grills got, the more sales we got.

In all, we did eight long-form and one short-form infomercials over the years. We created and promoted different grills, different sizes, shapes and different features. We kept adding to and improving the product.

Consumers had a major say in what product improvements were made, and what new grills were released. For instance, many consumers wanted to see removable grill plates that could be placed in a dishwasher for easier cleaning. This was easier said than done.

The major benefits of the original George Foreman Grill were the built in heating elements in the top and bottom grill plates. This resulted in even heat distribution and a rapid heat up time which made the grill ready to cook on in minutes.

Removable grill plates that were dishwasher safe would separate the element from the grill plates and reduce performance. It took us almost 5 years to find a solution. Our adjustment to the grill kept the heat-up speed and even temperature. *The Next Grilleration,* the grill with removable plates, was launched with almost instant success.

Another example of grill improvement took place in France. The French consumer had a preference for "Blue Steak," meat charred black on the outside and blue inside. Our engineers created a "burst" button so that if you wanted your steak blue, you pressed the "burst" button. This would create a significantly increased temperature for 30 seconds and would sear the outside of the steak, but leave the inside blue. I didn't want blue steak, but we always listened to our consumers and it is was one of many reasons for our companies success.

We also kept improving the Infomercial show. Here is a link from a show we did in 1996. See George with some of his family about 9 1/2 minutes into the clip:
http://bit.ly/1996GrillInfomercial

One of my favorite shows was a "grill off" with George versus a famous chef. We had a judges panel, just like all the popular cooking shows today.

Here is another link from one of the first grill infomercials. In the show, we used a nutritionist, Cherie Calbom. She was a great believer in the grill and in juicing. Later, we created her own show and a product called Juicelady® which ran for several years:
http://bit.ly/GrillInfomercialPt2

We studied warranty card returns and the comments consumers made. We discovered that retired people loved the product because it made their meal quickly and left no mess. The grill took just minutes to clean. Retired couples bought larger grills for their sons and daughters who had children. They started loving the product too. The final breakthrough was with college students. It was the first purchase made by most college freshmen, even before their books.

One fabulous version we created was a small grill with a bun warmer section on top to warm buns while you cooked your burgers. The grills were made with see-through lids in different colors.

The colors matched the new IPod® that Apple® was introducing that year which were such a big hit. When our product manager presented samples sent to us by the factory at our sales and marketing meeting, we found out he was color-blind. He did not realize the lids were, in fact, in color. The samples were unanimously accepted by all at the meeting, and we thought it was our best yet.

We did a short spot with George. It was a really fun ad! We aired it during Super Bowl.
Check it out:
http://bit.ly/GeorgeForemanGrillSuperBowl

It was another big hit!

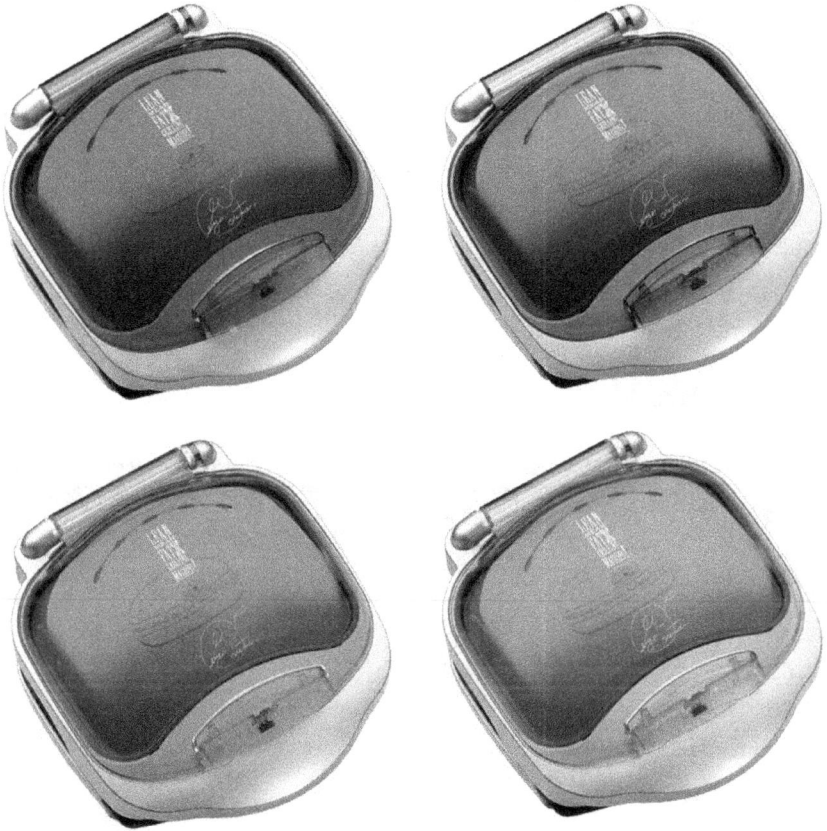

The bun warmer version

This link shows how popular the grill was with college kids; they took the time to make this video for fun.
http://bit.ly/712Studios

Here is the infomercial for the bun warmer grills:
http://bit.ly/ConceptsTV

.

George started getting bigger and bigger checks every month. His target of making a million dollars for the grill was eventually reached on a weekly basis at its peak.

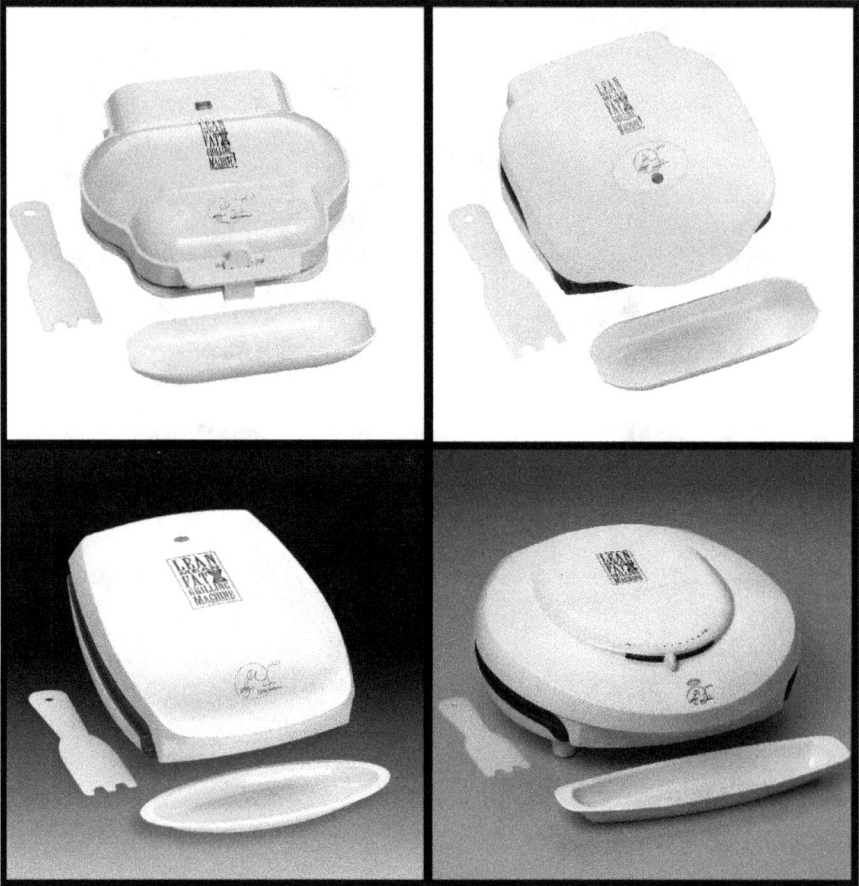

Grill Size Progression; the early years

Rick Cesari, started working with a very talented young man named Sean Fay. They produced the first Lean Mean Fat Reducing Grilling Machine infomercial. Sean now has his own company, Envision Response and he recently produced an infomercial I recommended him for; a new grill called *OptiGrill®* by *Tefal®*. I thought it will be a big hit, too.

The product is fabulous.
http://bit.ly/TefalOptiGriller

I was stunned with the demonstration. For years at Salton we talked to many engineers and asked them to develop a feature where the grill could measure if the steak was rare, medium or well done and then turn itself off when it got to the setting the consumer selected. Here it was and it worked perfectly. I admit I was impressed and jealous. I told all of the executives at Group SEB, owners of the Tefal® brand, this should be the next 100 million unit selling grill. It started being rolled out around the world under the name, T-Fal® Optigrill®.

It's available in the USA now.

PROMOTING THE GRILL

We learned from our Sandwich Makers and Juiceman® experiences that it was hard to keep a winning product on top for too long. Retailers get tired of the product and consumers just move on to something else. A better product comes along or it's simply a fad that goes out of fashion. That is the nature of this business.

So, the next few pages will be about things we did to keep the product rising in sales for almost 10 years. Then, I'll talk about how we kept it on the shelves as a staple; an evergreen for our retailers.

Here are some of my favorite things that kept us as the company that won more Innovation Retailers awards than the rest of this industry put together.

The Food Network did a one-hour show titled, *"George Foreman Campus Grill Off."* With George as a judge looking on, teams from Pepperdine, Missouri, Duke and Georgetown Universities cooked four rounds on the Grill. Each team prepared an appetizer, entrée, dessert and an innovative dish, using the grill in a whole new way. Prizes included scholarships, trophies and of course, lots of George Foreman Grills.

It was a fun show. The students were amazing and some of the recipes they developed can still be found online today. Missouri was declared the winner that day.
http://bit.ly/TheHoya

The Oprah Show

Oprah did a survey about 10 things people could not live without. Some of the answers were obvious. Wife, Husband, Children, Mother….
One of the things people could not live without turned out to be the George Foreman Grill. When Oprah heard this on her show, she was amazed. She kept saying with a questioning look on her face, "The George Foreman Grill??? The George Foreman Grill???" The audience was laughing. Oprah was laughing. But what kudos and sales for the George Foreman Grill.

Atlantic City

I only saw George fight once. This was in 1997 against Shannon Briggs in a World Championship fight. After 12 rounds, during which George hit Shannon with power punches so many times, we all wondered how Shannon was still on his feet.

George stood up in his corner during every break at the end of each round. I had already worked with George for 2 ½ years, so I knew him pretty well, but the George I saw in the ring was someone different all together.

This man was a warrior, a world champion, a legend and you could see why. The professional boxer that George is, was in the ring working and doing an unbelievable job at 47 years of age.

George lost that fight to a decision almost no one in the arena agreed with. When the announcement was made, the crowd kept booing and wouldn't stop. The announcer started interviewing George and the first question was about the decision.

"George" he said, "you clearly won the fight. What do you think about this terrible decision?" George responded that he had no issue with the decision. Shannon Briggs was a young man on his way up in his boxing career and everybody should support him to be a great champion. He certainly was proud to have fought him and wished him all the best for the future. By this time, the booing stopped. Then George said, "However, let me tell you about the George Foreman Grill."

The announcer stuttered, "George what has that got to do with the fight we are talking about?" "Look at me", said George, "See how much weight I lost preparing for this fight? See how healthy I am?" He pulled at the waistband of his shorts, showing how much more room there was now compared to before. "I owe it all to the George Foreman Grill. So make sure you go out there and get one for yourself ".

How proud I felt in seeing George in what turned out to be his last fight, transitioning into his new profession as a businessman and salesman extraordinaire.

Televised & Live Appearances

I really like Jay Leno. I have met him a couple of times and found him to be a kind and honest individual. He is a great standup comic who doesn't need profanities for his jokes to be funny. As host on NBC's *The Tonight Show,* he continued to stay on top for years without gimmicks.

George appeared many times on *The Tonight Show*. He cooked on the show several times using various George Foreman Grills and had everybody on the set eating and raving about the grill. Even Jay at times put on an apron and helped George grill and sell.

Hulk Hogan appeared on Jay Leno and said he had the choice to endorse the grill or a blender and chose the blender. I had no idea who had told Hulk this fairy tale. Maybe it was an agent looking for work. Hulk was great when we worked with him on a blender (the Thunder Mixer®), but as you read earlier in the book, George Foreman was the only one ever considered for the grill.

Appearances

There were appearances on the *Jimmy Kimmel Show*, *Entertainment Tonight*, *American Invent*or, CBS News, *Tony Danza Show,* CBS *The Early Show, ESPN Show and The Late Show with David Letterman,* just to name a few.

For five years, we were sponsors of the US Open Tennis Championships. The Men's Doubles were "The George Foreman US Open Doubles Championship". Over one million people attending the US Open were exposed to grill demonstrations, advertising, signage, George, George III and one time George Junior, handing out the trophy to the doubles champions. The Open was broadcast live all over the world.

At Santa Anita Racetrack
Photos provided by Rayetta Burr: Benoit Photo: benoitphoto.com

We also did small promotions too, like sponsoring a horse race in California with grills as giveaways.

George Foreman III, George Foreman, George Foreman Jr. and Tracy Austin at the US Open

Then again, George was a draw for many years before the Grill, appearing numerous times on the *Johnny Carson Show*, *American Bandstand, Hollywood Squares* and the *Sonny and Cher Comedy Hour*, just to drop some names to remind you how long he has been a star in one way or another.

CUSTOMERS

The George Foreman Grill was the biggest item in the housewares industry. Ever. The product was on allocation for the first few years. We simply could not produce enough to keep up with the demand.

Keith Hamden, one of our national sales managers, was given the responsibility of doing the allocations. This was no easy task.

We set up some guidelines for our customers which, in this business, means the retailers who buy in quantities from us.

Loyal customers who supported the company before George came on board were to be given priority. Customers who never bought from us in the past were on the bottom of the list.

Customers who could do in-store promotions, demonstrate the product, and had great advertising to support the product and feature it prominently in their catalogues, got priority.

Customers who only wanted the grill, but were not buying any of our other products, went to the bottom of the list.

Keith knew our guidelines, but it still was very difficult. He would get dozens of calls daily. Some would use flattery; others were threatening to never do business with us again. This was a very uncomfortable position for a salesman to be in.

Some tried going over his head and called me. This almost never worked. Keith had the responsibility and we made sure our customers knew it.

However, in some cases, the buyer was being chewed out by their boss for not having enough inventory and decided to phone me and "fix it".

Now, as you can imagine, this became even more delicate. You could burn a bridge that would cause the company major harm in the future. So, we made deals to create a win/win for both parties, but often, we simply had to say no.

I will come back to this supply and demand topic, but first let me tell you some of my favorite stories that happened with the grill and our customers.

Let's start with QVC®. This was a great customer for Salton®. We launched many products with this pioneering shopping network. The benefits were many. We got to test the sales potential of the product and what rate of demand we could expect.

We established the right retail price point, which was a critical factor in the life of any product. We watched the live, on air presentation and could see immediately what got the phones ringing during the presentation.

George made many appearances live on QVC®, at all hours of the day and night. QVC® loved George and he enjoyed being a guest there.

One day, George was on the set with two QVC® hosts presenting our latest grill. Both hosts got enthusiastic about the grill while talking to each other on air. George couldn't get a word in. So, as he was cooking burgers on the grill, he saw that some of them were ready; he made a burger and started eating it, not saying a word. I was in the studio control box watching this and all hell broke loose. There were flashing red lights and you started looking around to see where the fire was, but there was no fire. We went "red."

Going red at QVC® means all hands on deck. There are more calls coming in to place orders than there are telephone operators to answer them.

Flashing red lights send all other employees to the nearest phone to handle the overflow and take orders. QVC® is very good at what they do. As rare as this happens, they are still prepared to handle a situation like this and take care of their customers. They do not want to lose the customer who gives up when he or she can't get through.

What an exciting moment. All it took was for George to get hungry and start eating while the hosts were talking. I still smile when I think back to this moment. Over the years, QVC® sold millions of George Foreman Grills. We had a great relationship and mutual respect. When we went international with the grill, QVC® branches in the UK and Germany were the first customers to sell the product on air.

Then, there was Macy's®, the first customer to see the potential of the product before it got hot. The in-store appearances with George were truly exciting. Thousands of customers came for the opportunity to see George, maybe get the grill autographed, have a photo taken, or maybe just shake his hand.

George was fabulous in these appearances; he was very gracious to all, always stayed longer than promised, and was very conscious of not disappointing anybody who came out to see him. But, I can tell you this was exhausting work.

George had knee injuries and was often in pain standing for hours. He never complained, but you could see the relief on his face when he got in the limo after the appearance and could stretch his legs. Macy's stores were the best for celebrity appearances and merchandising events. They really knew what they were doing and we all walked away happy on both sides.

Then there was Sears® They wanted to do an exclusive George Foreman Grill and have George do a short-form infomercial for them to air. This was a great idea that almost did not get off the ground.

At a meeting in Chicago Sears® headquarters, while we were all discussing the details of implementing the idea, in walked their in-house attorney. As soon as he opened his mouth, I did not like him. He wanted independent studies done to confirm that grilling on a George Foreman grill did in fact "Knock out the Fat", and that what poured into the tray during the cooking process could, in fact, be called fat.

When I suggested that he open his mouth wide and I would pour the contents of the drained fat down his throat so he could decide if it contained fat or not, the meeting got pretty heated. The head of merchandising for Sears quickly realized this was going in the wrong direction and escorted the attorney out of the room. Barbara Westfield did have a study done in comparing how much fat George's grill "knocked out" compared to other methods of grilling.

The Lean Mean Fat Reducing Grilling Machine® was the winner in this independent study. I hoped the Head of Merchandising would pass it to the in-house lawyer, later, when I didn't have to see him again.

The exclusive grill was a major success at Sears®. Sears® used the formula of "short-form infomercials" on many other exclusive products with great success over the years. It was done with several Craftsman® tools and Kenmore® appliances.

The following year, Salton® won the annual vendor of the year award; the first time a small appliance company received it. We also earned several innovation awards from Sears® and got the chance to develop their entire Kenmore® small appliance range of products.

The Sears® team and the Salton® team had a great working relationship for years. It went so smoothly I only remember one other event during that time. Sears® had a store manager conference at their headquarters and asked us to bring George to speak. Over a thousand people were there. George won the audience over immediately.

Then, he told the story of how during his retirement he was running short of cash and needed to do some repairs to the Children's Youth Club he founded and took care of. So, he needed some tools and decided to buy them from Sears on credit. But, Sears refused to give him a Sears® credit card.

There was dead silence in the room. Then, George said he worked hard to develop the grill to be sold at Sears so he could finally get a Sears® card and asked if he could have one now! A roar of laughter filled the room and the managers went back to their stores in love with George and proceeded to sell a million grills during the first year.

Here is a photo of senior executives at Sears and the Salton team receiving the big Vendor of the Year award. I'm fourth from the left, Keith Hamden is fourth from the right' Barbara Westfield is on the extreme right, Mark Grand, second from the right, was GMM for Home, a wonderful fun guy and a great merchant. Richard Recklaus was the Senior Buyer, third from the left, with Barbara Pizzela (not pictured) as DMM. These three merchants were responsible for Sears doing this campaign so successfully. This was a lot of fun for all of us, not to mention the great memories.

Salton® gets vendor of the year award at Sears®

Since retail sales demand was created in part by our TV infomercials with George, price was very important. If retailers started using the grill as a loss leader to drive traffic into their stores and we were on air at a different price, TV advertising would stop working. Some retailers were not thinking long term business for the grill. They knew there was a huge consumer demand, so they saw it as an opportunity to drive traffic to their stores. Their way was to sell the product at cost or below; anything to beat other retail competitors. Yes this does work for them short term, but hurts the company that is creating new business with a great product and who are investing in this product for business longevity.

However, it is illegal to control pricing or do anything more than suggest a retail price. So the attorneys for Salton® were asked to develop a policy for us that would not break the law in any way, but protect our business from customers who "used" the grill for short term gain for them, but long term harm for us.

The attorneys developed a document called OAP policy. This stood for Order Acceptance Policy. We distributed it to all of our customers. The document said we understand the retailer has full right to decide what price to sell their product for, but we want our customer to understand that we also have the right to do anything to protect harm to our business. So, we reserved the right to refuse an order if we believed it could be harmful to our company. Boy, oh boy, did that cause an uproar with some retailers. Most loved it, but some were livid.

Walmart® did not take it well. In fact, during a shareholders meeting in Bentonville, Arkansas, one executive waved our letter in the air saying that nobody tells Walmart® how to do business or says no to Walmart®.

At that time, we were not doing business with Walmart® on any product. They asked to buy the grills, but we did not even have enough to allocate to our regular customers, so, we said no.

During a January International Housewares show in Chicago, Walmart® came to our booth and spoke to our Chairman, David Sabin. They brought with them an order for $100 million worth of George Foreman Grills, for delivery that year. David came out of the meeting and brought this news to me. He said, "What do you want to do here?"

We were a public company. There was a huge additional profit to be made here. Could we afford to say no to the biggest customer in the USA?

We said "no." We could not take the risk. Walmart® easily could sell at a price that would destroy our business elsewhere. We could not demand from them what price they would sell the product for. Walmart® was not buying anything else from us. We did not have enough product.

This was a very hard decision to make. It was tempting to take this windfall of profit, get a major boost to earnings for getting Walmart® as a new customer, and higher share price, but the benefit in my opinion, would be short lived and my partners agreed.

Later that year, David was asked to come and meet with a senior executive at Walmart® in Bentonville. The meeting started with the executive being aggressive. He insisted that nobody dictates to Walmart® and that Walmart® will always do what is best for them and suppliers have to live with it or not do business with them.

He then took his jacket off and said that was the Walmart® speech; now, with the jacket off, he wanted to speak as one merchant to another. He said they were getting hundreds of calls daily from store managers complaining they couldn't service Walmart® customers who came to the store looking for the George Foreman Grill.

He personally could assure Salton® that Walmart® would do what needed to be done not to hurt Salton® business, but to help Salton® grow their business. Based on this meeting, our production rate increasing each month, and the successful idea of having an exclusive model at Sears®, we said "yes".

We took a couple of models and gave them exclusively to Walmart®. Their first promotion on a day after Thanksgiving sold one million grills in one day. Our business relationship grew with Walmart®. They never harmed our business and did help us grow by buying many other products from our company.

In fact, they became our most profitable customer and the easiest to do business with. Yes, they were the toughest in negotiating price, but once a deal was struck, they always kept their word, honored all orders placed, and had the lowest product return rate and deductions of any customer out there.

I can't say the same about all of our customers. There were many funny stories with our customers, but the ones I have told are some of my favorites.

I just can't leave it with the domestic USA market retailer stories. There were great stories with customers in Australia, Brazil, South Africa, Germany, Spain, Holland, Ireland, Italy and New Zealand, to name some of the regions where George Foreman Grills were a success.

We kept building more grills to satisfy demand as quickly as we could. The factory that brought us the product and was producing it was increasing their space and hiring employees as fast as they could. They grew from having 800 employees when I first met them to a peak of 40,000 employees.

The factory moved to a new headquarters which became the largest space for small electrical appliance manufacturing in the world. I believed it was now time to take the grill international. The success of the grill sales in the USA was, however, old news by the time we started visiting retailers in other countries to offer our product.

Let me tell you about one of my experiences with the largest customer we had in the UK, Argos®.

Salton's staff in the office in Manchester, UK told me it was a waste of time to bring the grill to the UK. They believed other people had heard of the grill and tried over the years to introduce other versions in the UK that were known as "health grills." They failed miserably.

They also thought George, an American celebrity, was little known in the UK and would not be much use in promoting a grill. Finally, they said we don't eat burgers here, so why would any English consumers need a grill like this.

When I wanted them to try it anyway, they were stubborn and unwilling to do it. They believed they would be laughed out of the room and cause their stellar reputation harm.

So, I suggested they make an appointment for me with their biggest customer, Argos® and I said, "Let me try."

They smiled and were happy to let me try and thought I would make a fool of myself. Argos® is an amazingly successful, competent, and very smart retailer. Their buyers are some of the best-trained successful merchants I have met in the world. If they told me it would not work, I would need to move on and try another country.

At the meeting with three executives from Argos®, it started pretty much as our office told me it would. Health grills don't sell, we've never heard of George, and we don't eat burgers. But, I kept selling.

"George Foreman is unique and will be accepted warmly by the population here, the grill is healthy to cook many dishes with a burger being just one of them, we will support it with a major TV campaign." And on and on I went.

They listened to me politely, did not interrupt, and then put on the table what appeared to be a George Foreman Grill packaged identically to what we sold in the USA. A closer look showed the grill to be a 100% copy.

The picture was not of George, but a lookalike who turned out to be a famous UK rugby player. To make matters worse, it had a big sticker on the box: "CLEARANCE 50% OFF."

I could see the smile in their eyes when they looked at me and asked, "Do you still think your grill will succeed in UK?"

I did not blink an eye. "Yes", I said; "serves you right for buying a knockoff. People want the real thing, the thing with quality and a real endorsement, not a copy. You should have waited for us. So, please reconsider and buy our grill, the worst that could happen is that you will have a story to tell about this American know it all."

I also had to give them an IOU for satisfying some future request they had from our company. So, to be polite they ordered about 1000 units and promised to have it in their catalogue for Christmas. We saw other retailers and managed to get a total of about 6,000 units placed. It was not looking good.

I told our Managing Director, a veteran of the industry in the UK who was respected and liked by all, to order 250,000 units from our supplier in China. He said this was on me, and he would wash his hands from what will be a huge disaster. We'd have a warehouse full of goods sitting in the UK that nobody wanted.

Yes, I said, the responsibility would be on my shoulders. The next step was meeting with our advertising agency. I discussed a TV campaign, starring George. No long form infomercials were aired by anyone in this market. Cable was in its infancy and the public watched four national channels, one of them was the BBC, which had no advertising.

I said I wanted to spend 3 million pounds for the period leading up to Christmas. Again, in the wonderful polite English way, everyone told me that this was too excessive. The commercial could be seen as often as 15 times by a consumer, and they would be sick of it rather than enthused.

They also told me there was not enough airtime available to buy at this time of the year. We were new kids on the block and old customers would get the best space first. To cut the story short, we placed an order for one million pounds worth of media.

George filmed a 30 second commercial and the first year in the UK, we sold almost 2 million units. Retail sales were reported up because of the grill. The English public loved George and his appearances in the UK on television and on the radio. His press was memorable too. I got to say "I told you so," but between us, I was worried. Soon after the advertising started, Argos® called our company asking us to take the grill advert off TV. They could not keep up with enough inventory to satisfy the demand.

I will end the story with my second visit to Argos®. When I arrived in the lobby of their headquarters, I thought someone was selling tickets for charity. On a closer look, it was a pool by the employees to guess how many grills would be sold by Argos®. This had been going on for quite a few days with the number growing, big time, every day.

When the employees found out who I was, they all wanted to know how much of an increase of supply was coming to Argos before choosing their predicted sales number for the week. It was a great feeling to see the enthusiasm and excitement by all at Argos. Our company continued to develop what was already a great relationship before the grill. The business doubled and then doubled again. The European division grew from a 50 million to a 200 million pound business.

Sometime later the merchants of Argos® agreed to come to the United States to visit our showrooms and discuss what else we could do to continue growing our business. As they were landing in New York, the flight abruptly changed direction and no one on board was told what was going on.

It was the morning of 9/11. The flight was diverted to a Canadian Military base where they sat on the ground in the plane for hours. They saw soldiers entering the plane and escorting off a group of passengers of Middle Eastern origin. Eventually, they were told what had happened. They were allowed to leave the plane and for a couple of days stayed in the army barracks before they were allowed to continue to Chicago. On arrival in Chicago after their scary ordeal, their overnight stay at the Peninsula Hotel was greatly appreciated.

We had our meeting a few days late. One of the two ladies had expected a quick turnaround trip. Her mother was due to have treatment for cancer and she expected to be back in the UK well in time to be with her. On her return to the UK she asked Argos® to exclude her from any future travel overseas.

IT STARTED WITH ONE SMALL GRILL

Some of you think there is one George Foreman Grill in different sizes. Please take a look at this link and you will be astounded: **http://bit.ly/GrillsCompilation**

When we got to 88 different grills, I stopped counting. We had different sizes, colors, features and functions. There was something for everybody and every sales channel was tailored for our customers. We even made adjustments for the way various cultures cook around the world.

All these marketing activities surrounding George and the George Foreman Grill created a phenomenon the world took notice of. A perfect picture of this phenomena is in this CNBC Bizography they did about George as part of a series called *Titans*:
You can see it on Amazon instant video:
http://bit.ly/CNBCTitans

Bruce Walker was a valued member of the Board of Directors at Salton. He created an ever-green marketing book that featured the grill. He saw firsthand all that Salton and George were doing to make this brand and its products a success. He was co-author of a marketing book still in print today. The first item shown on the cover is the George Foreman Gril.
Available from:
http://bit.ly/BruceWalker

Many colleges used the George Foreman Grill story as part of their examples in business schools marketing courses. We would receive requests from students needing information and photos to use for their assignments. Our marketing department was always happy to answer their questions and send them what they needed.

GEORGE FOREMAN GRILL
ACCUSED OF BEING A MONOPOLY

We were a public company. Our top line sales and earnings were rising each quarter. We were reported as the third fastest growing company in USA. We were on the cover of business magazines. Ernst and Young gave us the Entrepreneur of the Year award. I was asked to appear on CNBC, Bloomberg and many other business shows.

In the late 90's, the price of our shares did a 3 for 2 split. The shares, while they kept rising, were still a very low multiple compared to the earnings.

I was very fond of almost all the employees at Salton. So with their annual review, one of their bonuses was options in Salton Shares. Options granted on a certain date are at the price the shares are trading for at that time. If the price rises in the future, the person holding options can buy more at the price they got them for and sell for the new higher market price.

With the options they got every year for being loyal and valued employees, coupled with the success of the company, there was a point where they were able to cash their options with big gains and pay off mortgages, send kids to college, buy a new car or create a better life for their families.

But while our price did keep rising and we did a 3:2 split (all shareholders received a free share for each two shares they owned), it did not sell at a multiple that other companies with similar results were trading at. A company was usually valued at a multiple of 12 - 16 times earnings per share and even more if the company was showing the type of growth Salton had.

Jim Chanos and his company Kynikos, a legendary short seller in financial markets, instead of investing in a company's success, would do the opposite. They bet the company would stop being successful or bet that it would fail completely. The share price would collapse. So they sell stock in a company they don't own (selling short) and when prices crash, they buy at the low price to cover the shares they sold but didn't own.

If, however, the price of shares keeps rising, they have to buy the shares at a higher price to honor what they sold but didn't own, taking a big loss. So "long" means investing for gains from the share price rising and shorts look for failure and shares going down in price.

But selling shares you don't own is a dangerous game. You only have a short time to deliver the shares you sold. So shorts "borrow " shares from traders who are holding shares for investors; their customers. These shares are borrowed for a fee, the broker makes a small profit and the owner of the shares often does not have a clue what is going on.

At one stage, nearly half the shares of Salton in the market were shorted. The war of longs versus shorts was something to watch. This was all about trading and had little to do with the company and its performance.

The longs started winning and there were no shares left to borrow to keep shorting. So the share price started rising rapidly. We hit a high of $62 after our 3:2 split. (Our share price was only 0.70 a short time earlier.) So an employee or a director who got 1000 options at 0.70 received a 3:2 split and was now able to buy the options for $700 and sell them for $93,500.

But out came a lawsuit against our company initiated by the Attorney General (later Governor) of New York, Eliot Spitzer. The lawsuit claimed we had a monopoly of the grill market and had engaged in unfair trade practices by withholding sales to some customers. All other states joined in the suit shortly afterwards.

The suit claimed that while we were following federal law, state law had a different interpretation of our OAP (Order Acceptance Policy) when a monopoly existed.

We could not understand this on so many fronts.

1. Federal Law language clearly allowed companies to do business with whom they chose. Elliott Spitzer claimed State Law had a different interpretation.
2. Monopoly on the grill market. Really? How about grilling on your outdoor gas grill, your charcoal barbecue, your griddle, your tabletop grill, your broiler etcetera.

3. Why would the Attorney General of New York make such a big deal out of this, especially as there were no retailers headquartered in New York who were refused supply of George Foreman grills?

Our Stock price started crashing hard overnight.

The suit continued for a couple of years and several million dollars in legal fees. Stock price continued to drift down. We were planning to do a secondary stock offering to support our growth. This was no longer possible. Investors would not take a chance in buying into a company with a law suit of this size hanging over the company's head.

To finance our growth we had to issue high interest bonds. We planned to repay this with a secondary offer later when the lawsuit was decided.

The shorts were delighted. Jim Chanos company, Kynikos, one of the biggest shorts in Salton, went from potentially losing a lot of money to a major gain almost overnight.

Our business at the same time was great, we were one of the fastest growing companies in the country, and we were employing more people and felt good about our success and prospects going forward. But this attack was so unexpected, hurting the morale of the Salton® team over time and it also became a distraction from focusing on the things that made our business the success it was.

It was settled after almost two years, requiring senior management to attend a lecture for three hours with a trade practices attorney. It also required our company not to supply a customer with grills for a minimum of one year after stopping shipments of the grill to them. That's it! An enormous waste of effort by all for what appeared to be no reason.

You may be baffled by this ruling not to ship a retailer for 12 months after stopping. So let me explain. If a retailer undermined our marketing campaign and the MSRP (Manufacturing Suggested Retail Pricing) we had in our advertising campaigns, we could not discuss this with a retailer but we could put allocations to that retailer to the bottom of our list. This would result in the retailer not getting supply for say 30-90 days. A retailer is likely to start running out of inventory and for certain would understand why he is on the bottom of supply availability. Once he starts getting shipments again, damaging our business would be weighed against damaging their own. Usually things settled down and all was well. With a ruling that now demanded that if we put a retailer at the bottom of our allocation list for a 12 month period, the dynamics changed dramatically. A retailer would not wait 12 months and was likely to buy a competitive product to sell as an alternative to George Foreman Grills. This would open the door for our competitors. The retailer would also be very angry not to get goods for that long and this would be very damaging for a long term relationship. The retailer may decide never do business again with Salton on any product. So we had to change our distribution strategy and focused on Channel Management by creating exclusive models for all major retailers. Holding shipments was no longer an option.

Soon after, I received a letter in the mail from Jim Chanos asking me to buy a table for $10,000 to a dinner he was to be co-chair of to raise funds for a "Re-elect Elliot Spitzer' campaign." We did not contribute.

Eliot Spitzer did become governor of New York. His political career was sunk when he was caught with a high-priced hooker, Ashley Alexandra Dupre.

What was even more shocking, was when somebody forwarded an article to me from the NY Post, March 16th, 2008 edition, written by Lukas Albert. The story was titled, "Eliot's Gal, A Shared Asset." The article said that Ashley was a party pal of one of Eliot's top financial backers, Jim Chanos, a billionaire hedge fund manager who runs Kynikos Associates in Manhattan.

All I could say, remarkable coincidences.

Then there was a series published July 1, 2009 by "Deep Capture" about Jim Chanos. I learned a lot from reading it.

Various articles on the matter appear here:
http://bit.ly/DeepCaptureGS
http://bit.ly/DeepCaptureSD
http://bit.ly/EliotsGal

BUYING THE GEORGE FOREMAN NAME

As our manufacturing grew and we were beginning to catch up with the demand, we would need to come down in price to appeal to new audiences and new products needed to be introduced with more features for new replacement business. Advertising and promotional expenses were going to rise in markets expected to be hard to win over. So, the profit sharing formula needed to change for us to be able to make the necessary investment.

I met with George and explained our plans to continue the success of the grill. I told him we beat his forecast of making a million dollars from selling the grill that first year. As a matter of fact, there was one month where the share of profit was almost $4 million, but it could stop as quickly as it started if we did not manage it right and prolong success.

I suggested that a win for all parties could be worked out. We would buy the George Foreman name for kitchen products in perpetuity for $100 million. We would repay this over a period of 5 years. This would be a capital gains transaction as we were buying his name. We would give George some shares in Salton to maintain his partnership and allow him to participate in the potential upside of the company going global with the grill. Pro-Rata, we would buy out Sam Perlmutter and Mike Srednick who had shares and were the original conduits in this venture.

We shook hands and the deal was done. Later, I found out George was happy with the deal, but sad at the same time. He loved selling the grill. He felt this deal was the end of it. When George saw the documents however, that also included an agreement for him to continue for the next 5 years to promote the grill, he was happy. At the end of the 5 years, it was extended for another 2 years. George continued working tirelessly and did everything to promote the grill.

This was the largest deal at that time for the endorsement of a sporting figure.

Five years passed and the total was paid out. Shares were sold at a major gain and it was clear to both of us that this worked out the way it was planned. Sam Perlmutter and I still continue our friendship and meet every year, happy this deal worked out so well. Mike Srednick passed away a few years ago from a malignant brain tumor, but he is fondly remembered by us all for all time. I miss him often.

Photo courtesy of HomeWorld Business/ICD Publications

No matter how much success there is in your business you can't rest on your laurels. I always looked at more deals and tried to predict the next big thing.

GLOBAL PROMOTIONS WITH GEORGE

I asked Samantha Dreimann, who travelled with George all over the world, about some of her appearances with him in the United States, the UK, Germany, the Netherlands, South Africa, Brazil, Dubai, Australia, Hong Kong, Mexico and anywhere in between.

As one of the marketing managers at Salton, she was given extra duties, not only because she was very good at it, but George was happy and thought of her as one of the family. They remain close to this day.

She not only made all the arrangements for George's travel, accommodations, limos and security, but she dealt with our offices around the world in scheduling appearances for George. Even more importantly, she was the liaison with all forms of media who wanted George for TV, radio and press interviews. There was always more demand than available time, so she had to choose what would be best for all of us without hurting anyone's feelings.

I was there on many visits. It was a thrill to see George welcome everywhere. The visits seemed to be so perfectly planned. But there was always drama behind the scenes. Always. TV appearances would run over time; others would start late or needed to be rescheduled.

Samantha was glued to a phone. Over the years, first it slid apart, then it flipped, then she got a Blackberry (all of this was before 'smart phones'). Files and schedules jammed under another arm, making it all work.

Here are some of her memories of travels around the world with George and the Grill.

PART II:

LEARNING FROM GEORGE

BY SAMANTHA DREIMANN

I was born and raised in Melbourne, Australia. All through my childhood and into my teens, I enjoyed creating things and teaching myself new skills. By the age of 16, I was designing and making clothing and accessories and selling them in Melbourne.

Bored with school, I left before I was 17 and worked in retail for 5 years, selling everything from swimming pools to men's swimwear. Before turning 21, my photo appeared in the entrance of the David Jones Sydney city store with the caption "Salesperson of the Month." You can see that sales and creativity runs in the family.

Following my interest in design, and with Leon's help, I applied to attend FIDM, The Fashion Institute of Design and Merchandising in Los Angeles, CA, where I studied Fashion Design in 1992/93. After graduating, I worked for a local designer sourcing fabrics, working with local manufacturers to have the garments made, as well as selling the fashion line. I grew the business, which panicked the designer, as the more you sell the more you have to spend. It made her nervous so I moved on to my next gig.

I worked for a while at a Sears store in their Visual Display Department. I had zero experience in dressing mannequins and doing this type of job but they hired me right away based on walking me around the store and my advising them what I would do for each department to make things look more saleable. I was however a little taken aback when I was asked to dress the male mannequins in the juniors department to appeal to gangs in the area. This was before we had the internet to do research so I just studied the customers and did my best.

All of this experience in Melbourne and Sydney, Australia and then in Los Angeles, USA, gave me the experience and knowledge I needed to become a part of the Salton team in Chicago, IL. My retail experience gave me the knowledge I needed to get Salton's first retail outlet up and running at a mall called Gurnee Mills and the design experience helped me create product lines for various housewares brands.

My first introduction into creating lines of kitchen electrics, personal care and seasonal items also came with an education in product licensing. Salton had teamed up with Applica (a personal care and housewares company in Florida) to sign a license agreement with White Westinghouse to use that brand on product lines to be sold exclusively to Kmart.

Leon took me to visit suppliers in Hong Kong as well as to factories in China. He gave me a quick lesson on product sourcing, suppliers and doing business in Asia. It was a little similar to what I had done in Los Angeles but on a much, much larger scale.

About a year after joining Salton, the grill entered my life. Day to day activities which had formerly consisted of license negotiations, product sourcing, trade shows, product design and development, sales meetings and more for several brands, now had an extra element to them and I needed more hours in the day the more successful the grill got. I became the go between person between George, Salton and anyone wanting to talk about the grill.

Early on, one of the best things I learned from George was that he would never say something bad about another product, even one trying to compete with his. He believes that if a product is good, it should be able to stand on its own and not be sold based on putting down another product. This is something many advertising agencies, especially infomercial companies, have a hard time understanding or accepting, but it is something that I find truly admirable in a person who puts his name on a product.

Sam and George in the 1990s

George would always travel with someone from his family. When we first started hitting the road on promotional jaunts, one of his nephews usually came along, one of whom is also called George. The other was a very tall policeman from Texas; both of whom were as intimidating in size as George, but also like George, teddy bears underneath. It was like traveling with my own personal security crew.

Nephew George had the thickest Southern accent I have ever encountered and Big George, as George Foreman is often called, would usually have to translate for him. I'm an Aussie gal, and he never once batted an eyelid at my lack of southern accent comprehension.

Once George's children were old enough to learn the business, graduated from college or were on school break, they started traveling with George, one at a time, to learn from their dad, work for him and assist in the daily event scheduling and business side of their dad's life. This was not a taking your kid to work day snooze. They put in the hours, worked hard and received valuable on the job training.

Early on, Georgetta Foreman was my go-to-gal to work with on scheduling her dad for our promotional activities. She was with us during our first public relations visit to Germany where George presented the grill on QVC whilst we where there. Before long she was married, had a family of her own and started working in television production and working up ideas for new TV series. Georgetta always has a smile on her face making everyone feel at ease, just like her dad.

Natalie Foreman joined us on a future visit to Germany and was brought into the festivities by having to learn some German whilst we where there.

George III and I spent so much time working on his dad's schedule and traveling together that I really did feel like his big sister at times and still do. George III has now spread his wings and become quite the entrepreneur himself. Monk, as he is known to his family and friends, opened a fitness center in 2014, in Boston. Monk is driven like his dad and has put the hours and effort into making The Club by George Foreman III a total success. When I see The Club and talk to Monk it is clear that he learnt so much from Big George and maybe even a little something from the Dreimanns. There will probably be an infomercial in his future. Fitness videos are already in the works.

George Jr. worked with us as well for a year in the marketing department at Salton learning what we did during our day to day marketing and business activities. Being the eldest son he was sometimes called on when his dad couldn't be present, to do things like give an award at a business or promotional function. In true Foreman tradition he was a professional through and through.

Later on it was my pleasure to work and travel with George IV who still assists his dad today with various business activities. Our last business trip was to Canada where Big George filmed a commercial for Canadian Tire and the George Foreman Cleaning Solutions whilst George IV and I stood on the side lines wondering if the small horse on set would like the big guy (George). This wasn't the first time I had George on a set with live animals. Big Wheel, as George IV is also known, and his brother George Jr. manage their dad's company called Foreman Boys Promotions. A fight promotion company making sure matches are fair and fighters are protected.

Boxing has become a bit of a family affair. Even Freeda Foreman got into the ring a few times. Freeda Foreman worked with us on an infomercial with her dad. He cooked on and spoke about the grill and Freeda demonstrated and spoke about the Salad Express™, a device to make a great salad which was the perfect accompaniment to the protein cooked on the grill. Soon after Freeda left the world of boxing we made an infomercial with her called Freeda Foreman Family Fitness. There was a pack up that focused on family activities, exercise, cooking a healthy diet; ways to bring families together through health and fitness.

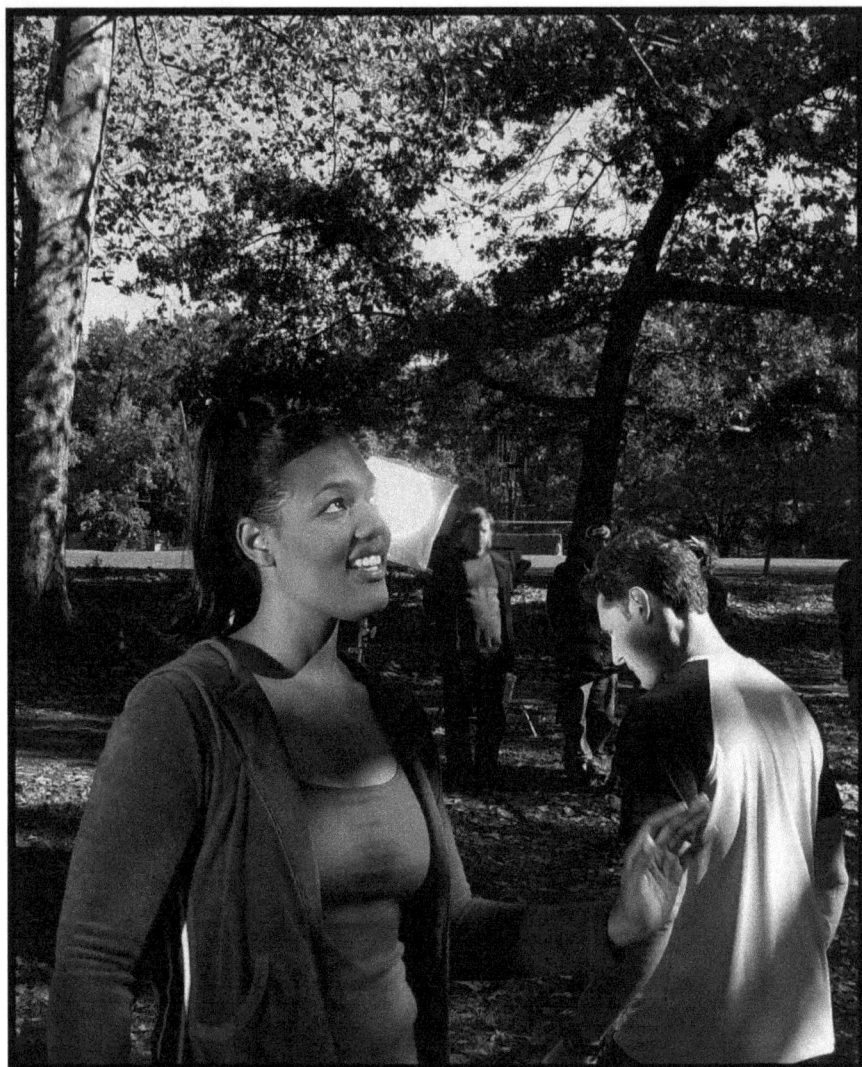

Freeda Foreman filming a fitness video
(with Jaime Brenkus in the background)

George III - Business Entrepreneur:
http://everybodyfights.com/

We traveled around the USA and then around the world promoting the grill for 13 years. George always made me feel like a part of his family. I heard stories and saw the movie, *Rumble in the Jungle,* about this tough boxer from his earlier years, but I have never seen a trace of that man. It is hard to imagine him then, knowing him now. George is a family man, a jokester and a friend who takes the high road in any circumstance.

"THE COOKING MAN"

As George was seen more and more often in infomercials, commercials, talk shows and various media channels, a new fan base was born.

He was no longer George Foreman the boxer, the heavy weight champ or the Olympic Gold Medal winner; he became known as the "Cooking Man' to this younger generation who didn't know what professional boxing was.

Everywhere we traveled young children would see George and whisper to their parents, "That's the cooking man." George would let out a big smile and whisper back, "I was the heavy weight champ you know."

George loved these young kids who knew him as a cook, and like a good politician, he would always stop and have his photo taken with them. The older kids would want George to high five them or shake his hand for their photo memento their parents were waiting eagerly to snap.

Sometimes George would put the toddlers on his shoulder or he would cradle the small babies in his arms. No matter where we were, George would always take time for his fans and the children no matter if they knew him as a boxer or a cook.

Hasbro® was the first to see an opportunity born out of the grill and George's popularity amongst children and parents. They approached us about a licensing agreement to make a toy grill using George's name on it. We negotiated a license agreement with Hasbro® which resulted in Salton and George having a 50/50 split of the deal. The toy grill design was shaped like one of the original grills with the colored bun warmer lid.

By mimicking the bun warmer version of the grill, they were able to launch the product in several colors to appeal to children. The Hasbro® toy grill was part of their Play-Doh® line and even made a sizzling sound when you pressed down on the lid.

Hasbro® Toy Grill®

By including Play-Doh® and molds, children could mold their own food and pretend to cook it. Parents loved it almost as much as their children did. Whilst parents prepared dinner for their family, their young ones prepared a Play-Doh® version alongside them in the kitchen, bringing the whole family together, where they could be heard saying, "What should we grill with George tonight?" or "Can you pick up some steaks to grill on George?"

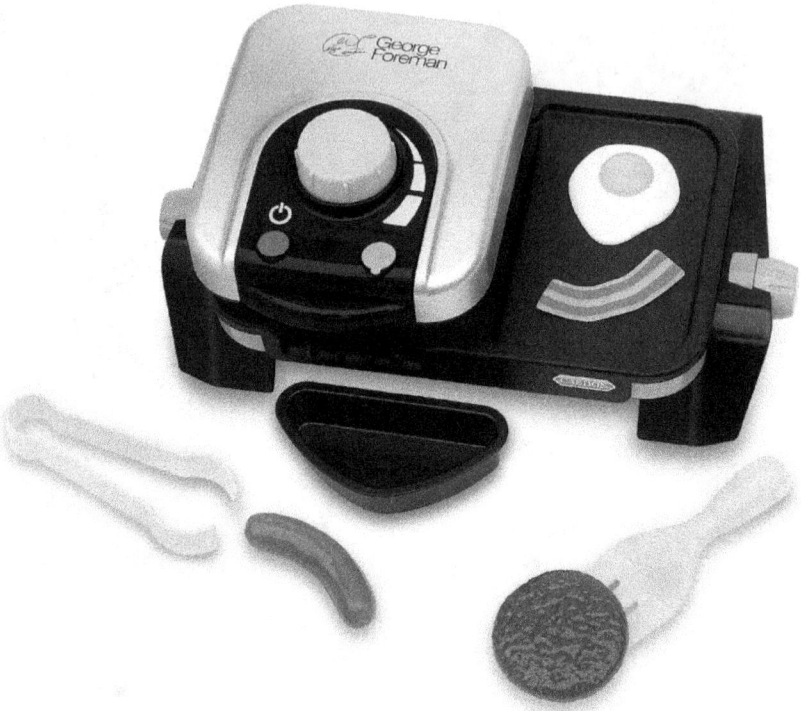

Casdon® Toy Grill

A few years after Hasbro® released their version of the toy grill, a company called Casdon® Toys in the United Kingdom also launched a version for the UK market.

Not only did the toy companies see an opportunity to seize the Foreman name but other industries wanted to capture sales from this hot new commodity as well.

Franco Manufacturing Co. Inc. who specializes in many licensed products in the soft goods Housewares Industry, licensed the brand from Salton and George for a line of textiles. I negotiated the deal and took care of the approval processes just as I had done with Hasbro®.

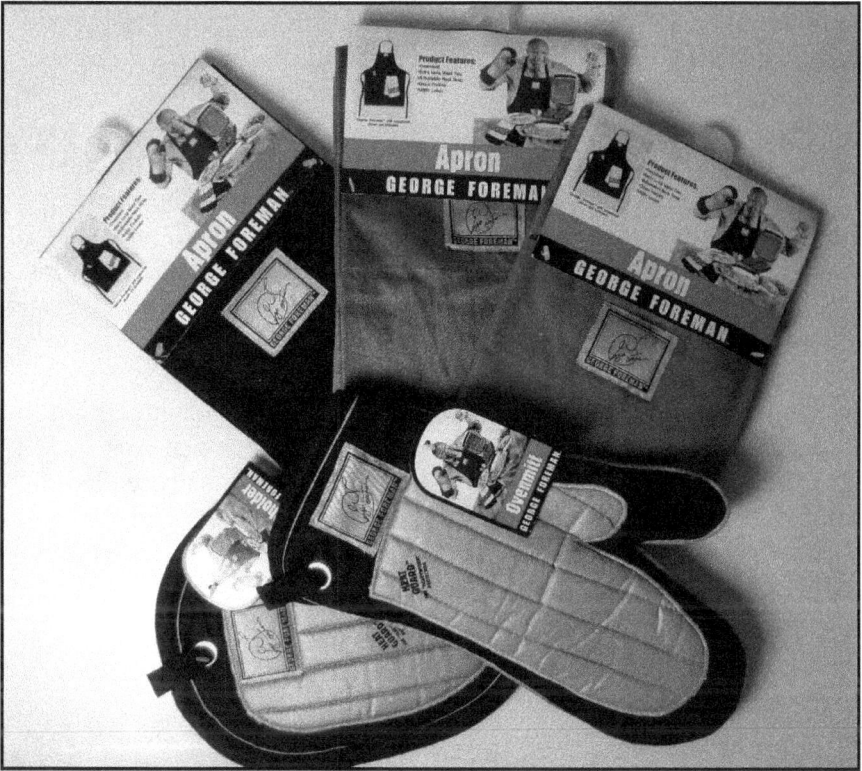

Franco Manufacturing licensed product

The products included aprons, dish towels, oven mitts, heat pads and more. They even designed and made grill covers for the most popular grill sizes for people who wanted to leave their grills on the counter but covered. We made sure to use the items whenever possible during grill product demonstrations and print or film adverts to ensure full brand exposure for the brand and the licensee.

The grill took on a new identity as a part of the family home and an integral part of day-to-day cooking. To this moment, I do not know of another appliance given a human name.

As the grill became known as "George", in 2002 a 30-second television commercial was created called "I grill with George." Various scenes show people from a fireman to a mother and son saying, "I grill with George." By listening to the public and tapping into what they thought of the product and how they used it, we could create advertising around this information.

Even Australians got into calling the grills George and feeling like George was a part of their meal time. A famous skit was performed down under by Rich Hall on a television show called Spicks and Specks. He made up a song which, in part, said, "If you won't cook my dinner, George Foreman will."

"Free Advertising" and Pop Culture

The grill, or "George" as it became known, was such a household name that the product started showing up in positive ways in movies, television shows, scripts and as part of comedy routines.

Positive, free advertising is what anyone selling a product dreams about, and it just kept coming. Even the makers of Trivial Pursuit® contacted us to use George and the grill as one of their questions in one of their DVD versions of the game.

In 2009, Mariah Carey got in on the pop culture obsession that is George Foreman and the Grill. Her song *Obsessed* has lyrics, which say, "He's all up in my George Foreman," which, I was led to believe, is a way of saying someone is in your face. It was explained to me like this: George Foreman equals grills, and grills are a reference to the decorative retainers some people took to wearing in their mouths. These grills are usually made out of gold, silver or even diamonds. So, if someone is in your grill, they are in your face, hence "in your George Foreman."

Prior to Mariah's *Obsessed*, Nelly released a song in 2005 called *Grillz*, in which there is a line, "Call me George Foreman because I'm selling everybody grills." Yes, the song is about the teeth retainers but an interesting use of George and the grill in this rap song. Whoever would have thought that a kitchen appliance would make it into song lyrics?

I have read where people have made assumptions that product placement fees were paid because the grill showed up in so many places. That is untrue.

George and the grill became a part of pop culture; an icon, a symbol people knew, could relate to and understand. Jokes sprang up around the grill too. My favorite was about a man divorcing his wife. When the Judge asked him what he wanted of the assets, he said "All I want is my George Foreman Grill."

In an episode of *Sex and the City*, fajitas are cooked on the grill and the product name mentioned in its entirety. In *The Big Bang Theory*, Amy mentions the grill as well as gives the sales pitch about it sealing in the flavor without the fat.

There are George grill mentions and references in such shows as *The Office* (United States version), by Ellen DeGeneres during her *Saturday Night Live* monologue and so many more. *Law and Order SUV* even opens one of their episodes with two policeman on horses talking about the grill. Long after George stopped promoting the grill himself, it still gets mentioned in the most unusual places. In A&E's show *Storage Wars*, Barry Weiss pulls a suntan bed out of a locker and says, "It is a George Foreman tanning grill; A lean, green tanning machine."

George has also been asked to appear on television shows that promoted the grill. His likeness appeared on *King of the Hill*, where an animated George is seen with George doing the voice over for it. George's animated character gets a little crazy when the grill is called a novelty item by another animated character on the show.

Many people have seen or heard about the goodie bags celebrities get at various events. Often suppliers donate products for these bags, for a fee, and many set up a booth in a tent, for a larger fee, in hopes that celebrities will stop by their table and have their photo taken with their product.

I was never one to easily agree to pay for placement, but I could be convinced to give away product for the right occasion. In 2002, we donated grills to the Country Music Awards, Soul Train Music Awards and the Latin Billboard Awards for their celebrity product showcase.

The company who set up the showcase put the grills on the table for celebrities to see and take home with them. They also took two out of their boxes and asked the musicians to autograph them. As a result, we received two large grills back and a booklet showing photos of some of the celebrities who signed them. These grills were on display in our showroom for staff and visitors to see. Grills were autographed by Kid Rock, Nelly, Ja Rule, Marc Antony, Nancy O'Dell, Montgomery Gentry, Toby Keith and many more.

On Campus

As the years rolled by and more and more grills were sold, the marketing became a topic of many school papers. We often received emails and phone calls from students who wanted to know the history of the grill and wanted more information on George and his part in the success. We gladly provided answers to all of their questions to help with their assignments. We were always amazed as the free publicity kept coming in, sometimes in unlikely forms.

The grill also became a college dorm room staple. It was the "must have" item to the point it was mentioned in the college welcome packet at universities. Some schools had it on the "allowed" list while others made sure it was on the "not allowed" list of items students could have in their room. The lists mentioned the product by name, not as a generic appliance.

The grill became a part of college life. Late night grilled cheese sandwich? Cook it up on George.

With the explosion of social media, now everyone can share their grill stories and recipes. Some students blog about the grill. They give advice to freshmen such as how you can save money by not eating out all the time and use the George Foreman Grill to cook everything from burgers to fajitas in their campus apartments. George Foreman boards have shown up on Pinterest with people sharing their favorite recipes.

Now with popularity of hashtags you can search #georgeforemangrill on places like Instagram and Twitter to see photos of what people have cooked on their grill, recipes they are sharing or just posts from people letting the world know they purchased a grill.

A YouTube search for the grill will show videos from the serious cooking demonstration to spoofs of the infomercial. Ideally, capturing the interest of students who see a product as a way of life, will create a customer for life. I'm sure the George Foreman Grill has done just that.

USA

When we first launched the grill in the USA, George made store appearances across the country from San Francisco to New York. People came out in droves and lined up to meet the champ and get his autograph whilst product demonstrators grilled up a variety of foods around him to show how easy the product was to use. People in line were provided with food samples to taste and ease their waiting time.

George would sit there for hours, signing postcards, or the photos we supplied, or paraphernalia the fans would bring with them. He smiled that cheeky smile of his for anyone wanting to take a snap shot, and he took the time to pose with some fans in a boxing position or put his arm around them. The media also turned up to witness this boxer showing up in the cooking section of a department store. Reporters had to see firsthand this crazy match between a boxer and an electric grill.

After our first store appearance in San Francisco at the Macys Valley Fair Mall, I recall turning on the television in my hotel room to watch the KPIX Channel 5 evening news and was shocked to see myself on the screen in the background of a news report about George being in the city to promote his new grill. This was news?

Photos and articles about George and the grill started to show up in newspapers. *The New York Times* covered George when he appeared at Macy's in New York. Channel 7 News put him on the evening report when he made an appearance at the Marshall Field's Flagship store in Chicago. The reporter called him 'The People's Champion.'

George signing autographs at Marshal Fields, Chicago, IL USA

The only time I saw a fan get out of hand during a store appearance was in New Jersey. We were in the parking lot getting into the car when a male came running towards us, arms flailing in the air. I'll admit to being a little concerned about this person's intentions and may have yelled at George to get in the car quickly (not that he couldn't take care of himself, but I am protective of the big guy). Security jumped in front of the fan and calmed him down.

He was just eager to get George's autograph and had been running late for the store appearance. George, of course, gave the fan his autograph, which made the fan's day, I'm sure.

Yes, the grill was great and it worked as promised, but George's charisma and the way consumers embraced him was definitely part of the package and part of the grill success story around the world. He wasn't just a spokesperson; he truly believed in the product and people believed in him. Others tried to duplicate the teaming of a product and a celebrity, but George is one of a kind and cannot be duplicated.

In the early days, soon after launching the grill, during a store appearance in the Macy's New York Cellar, I was approached by a representative from the Conan Show. Conan was relatively new to the late night talk show circuit. He'd only been on air for a couple of years and we were new to promoting the grill on talk shows. Given this was all unknown territory to me, I went with my gut and rolled with the flow. Arrangements were made to get George and a grill to the New York studio and a team was born; the team being George, Conan and the grill.

George became a frequent guest on Conan's show and Conan always welcomed him back with any new grills we were launching or whatever George was pitching. It became a tongue in cheek joke between them that George would pitch a grill or his latest book during the interview. Conan gained a new fan in me as he always played along, prompting George to make his pitch.

Once retailers understood what an integral part of their housewares sales the grill was, George was often invited to talk at manager's retail conferences or attend retail staff luncheons. Before such events, I would let George know the theme of the event: Team building, sales, management or whatever the retailer had in mind for the day.

George, having a very busy schedule, didn't seem to prepare for these events. Five minutes before he had to go on stage, I would remind him what the theme of the day was and what the speech should be about and he blew me away every time.

George could get on stage and give a speech that was always relevant to the topic of the day. Sometimes these conferences were so large that he would give his speech, then the room was cleared, and another couple of hundred people were ushered in, and he would give them a totally different speech. These speeches often ended in standing ovations from a newly acquired group of fans, all new believers in 'The Power of George.'

During one of these managers' lunches at Sears, Martha Stewart was also in attendance. I could hear management talking about how they wanted to introduce George and Martha to each other, but she was in another room a bit of a walk away and they were unsure who should go to whom.

Overhearing their conversation, I asked George if he would like to meet Martha. George, ever the gentleman, got up and we headed to where she was. No discussion. No celebrity fuss.

As George and the grill's popularity grew across the nation, so did the media requests for George. We didn't have a PR company pushing any of this; it just happened naturally and the phone requests kept coming in.

One year, I set up radio interviews across the country. George had been interviewed on one radio show then after that, my phone kept ringing. The more interviews he did, the more people heard him on air and the busier my phone line got. I coordinated phone interviews where either George would call the station at a pre-arranged time or they would call him. For a while there, he was doing several interviews a day, many days of the week, throughout the year. George and his tales of the grill could be heard on radio talk shows all across the USA.

The most memorable of these interviews was with Man Cow. Man Cow is a well-known disc jockey in Chicago with a wild reputation. This radio interview booking gave me cause for concern. I have always respected 'George the Preacher' and as such, stayed away from reporters who were let's say, unsavory.

Man Cow's people were practically pleading to have George on air for an interview so I made them swear that Man Cow would not say anything rude, out of line, or basically behave badly, which was what he was known for. On the morning of the call-in, I sat by the radio holding my breath, hoping I had done the right thing in trusting these people.

I still laugh about this interview today because it was so vanilla, George must have wondered if it was a prank call. Man Cow could not have been any Godlier or well-behaved than he was that day. Even I wondered who was on the air and Man Cow's listeners must have been confused as well.

As I looked back through some of my files I noticed that in 1999 George had fully embraced using email whereas we at Salton had not yet been set up with it. I was using an AOL email address on an account which I was sharing with Leon. Given email was still in its infancy we just had the one account. Many people in business were still using faxes to communicate. Leon and I would often bump each other off line or I had to check to see if the account was free for me to sign on. Not only were we in the early days of email we were also using a dial up connection.

STEVE AND DC

THE POWERHOUSE, ST. LOUIS, MO 63103

Thank you so much for setting up our George Foreman interview! It was great talking to George. Please keep us in mind for future interview possibilities!

Dean & Nick
PEAK 95.1 KRDO

KRDO
AM · FM · TV · KSKX FM

Sam,   July 27, 1999
  Just a quick note to thank you so much for your help with our interview with George Foreman. He was an absolute doll! If I can ever do anything for you in the future please don't hesitate to call!
          Thanks again! Stacy

93³FM FLZ

Hey! Sam! Many Thanks! Joey B!

Subj: **Re: FRIDAY RADIO**
Date: 7/30/99 2:26:24 PM Central Daylight Time
From: George
To: Sam

Well, my dear friend we had good week; I can't believe it I am up every morning, I got a job.
I hope they like it.
Thanks for all the hard work
George

In addition to being a regular guest on Conan, George appeared on the Jay Leno show and even had a segment with Jay showing him how to cook on the grill. He also cooked with Tony Danza on the *Tony Danza Show*, two men, grilling side by side in front of a live audience. Tony really got into the grilling and was great at pitching the product along side of George. With Jay, it was a little more of a comedy routine but still great publicity either way.

As the internet grew in popularity, requests for different types of interviews came in. Even bloggers got on board writing about the grill. NPR interviewed George and the broadcast became one of their most popular interviews at the time; for months people talked about the interview they could listen to on the web over and over again.

This was before Facebook, Twitter and all the other media avenues we have today. Imagine how much bigger and faster growing the grill popularity would have been in the 90s with today's social media sharing. It's mind blowing. George was always being asked to appear on a variety of television talk and news shows. He was always willing and made sure to plug the grill no matter what the interview subject was about. If he could turn a boxing loss into a promotion for the grill, he could do anything.

2004 George cooking on the street in New York

In 1997, Foreman versus Briggs was a talked about match in which a controversial decision named Briggs as the winner much to the amazement of anyone watching the match including those observers ringside. When George was interviewed by the ring moments after the match, he went into a sales pitch about the grill. Reporters and radio show hosts asked and wrote about this grill sales pitch probably as much as the match itself.

George even cooked live on the *NBC Today Show* on the street outside of the NBC New York Studios. His fans watched in person and on their television.

The G5 commercial was memorable and a fun 30-second spot to film. The G5 had 5 removable plates so you could make waffles or omelets, use as a griddle and of course, as a grill. We filmed the commercial in Houston, Texas with a New York City advertising agency that had to truck in special equipment from Los Angeles which had the technology to achieve the spot. The premise was there were 5 removable plates, so 5 Georges would be seen on the screen talking to each other. It sounds a little schizophrenic but the end result was very good.

For thirteen years, George talked about his life and promoted the grill to anyone who asked about it. During this time if you picked up a newspaper or a magazine or turned on the television or listened to the radio, you were sure to hear or see George and one of the many versions of his famous grill.

As new grill variations were launched, so were new ways of promoting them. On shows such as *Ellen DeGeneres* when she had her Twelve Days of Christmas promotion, grills were given away to lucky audience members. So, it wasn't a car like Oprah's audience received, but Ellen's fans were happy.

Show hosts and reporters across the country and then the world were always given a grill to take home and try for themselves. I am sure this helped with the ever-increasing grill media mentions.

The variety of grills kept increasing, as did exposure and advertising efforts to show the different features of each new product.

In 1999, we had George Foreman Day at Wrigley Field in Chicago. Besides the man chasing after us to get George's autograph in New Jersey, this was the only other time fans have given me a slight cause for concern.

We pulled up in the stretch limo outside of the stadium and as close to the VIP entrance as possible. There was still a short walk to get to the door. Had I known what the crowd reaction was going to be, I would have chosen a much less conspicuous vehicle to arrive in. The VIP entrance is right next to the front gates of the stadium so the crowd saw the car, then they saw George get out of it.

Hundreds of people came charging towards us and my initial reaction, along with George's nephew who was with us that day, was to step between George and the Cubs fans. If we blocked them, it would give George a chance to get inside to safety and not be trampled.

What was I thinking? George was strong enough to hold them back with one arm, as was his nephew who was a policeman in Texas and much taller than George, but I stood between them, hands in the air in a STOP stance and told George to get inside. Once in the stadium, there was a VIP level where we were able to walk around, in view of the crowd but out of reach.

When the thousands of people in the stadium saw George, they let out mighty cheers and I was thankful we were on a secure level where we could be seen and not touched. We were escorted onto the field where the Cubs were warming up and John Cusack was with them dressed in a baseball uniform.

This was the first of several surreal celebrity moments for me when traveling with George. I wasn't sure why Cusack was in a baseball uniform warming up with the Cubs but no one else around me thought this was bizarre. John came over to George and they were just casually chatting while I stood close by.

At one point the actor just stared at me so long I said, "Hi, I'm Sam." Can you believe he didn't say a peep back? He just starred some more. Awkward.

George Foreman Day at Wrigley Field was a success and just one of the many unique ways we spread the word about the grill. George threw out the first pitch then sat with the commentators in the booth to watch the game and sing along to 'Take Me Out to the Ball Game."

Before the game started, whilst on the field, George made his way over to a group of young fans hanging over the fence, squealing for an autograph. George signed baseballs and programs for these young men who were decked out in their Cubs gear.

Unfortunately I wasn't permitted to go into the locker room, but George entered before the game and chatted with the players. Judging by the photos I saw after the event, the players were thrilled to have him there.

George Foreman Day at Wrigleyfield

George singing at Wrigley Field

George in Sydney, Australia

AUSTRALIA

We made visits down under with George three times to promote the grill between 1999 and 2006; twice to Melbourne and once to Sydney. The first year we visited Melbourne, George had 9 children and one on the way, so it is interesting to look back now and hear interviews with George talking about his 4 boys named George and then to hear the stories during future visits, which changed to 5 boys named George.

Australia has a very small population for the size of its land mass, so the fact that 750,000 grills were sold within the first few years of the product launch was pretty impressive. Keep in mind that in 1999, Australia was a tourist destination, but nothing like it is now.

Things we take for granted in the USA, like finding a stretch limousine for a celebrity airport pick up were a lot more challenging in Australia back then. Limousines were around but mostly rented for weddings not celebrity transport for a week. We did find one, but I think it was from the 1980s but it got us where we needed to go.

Now Australia is a go to destination for people like the Kardashians and Paris Hilton, looking to promote what they are selling or are being paid to promote. In the 90s and early 2000s, George was one of the few American celebrities to really tour down under to promote a product.

The Australian team at Salton® wanted to put an Aussie spin on their marketing efforts and created a product segment called 'Health Power', which included the grill and captured the hearts and minds of Aussies in pursuit of a healthy lifestyle and healthy cooking ideas. Australia has always been known for barbeques and meat eating, so letting locals know they could still cook and eat the same way but with less fat was a win/win for all.

To reach the people in the outback and small country towns, far away from the big city retail stores, a van was emblazoned with product labeling and driven to faraway places. Grills were literally sold out of the back of a van in rural areas to people who would otherwise have to drive hours to the closest store carrying the grills. They couldn't have been happier that the grill came to them. That old-fashioned ingenuity still works there today.

All the Aussie media wanted to interview George and for him to appear on their shows. Every time George appeared on air or in the pages of a newspaper or a magazine, the grill appeared with him. Reporters from newspapers such as *The Herald Sun* showed up to interview George about boxing and cooking. George was live on morning talk shows such as *Good Morning Australia* with Bert Newton, on *Dave & Kim* and on *The Today Show*. He appeared on daytime talk shows such as one with *Denise Drysdale*, on evening news shows with BBC International Broadcast and on Foxtel being interviewed by Sam Kekovich for *Pardon the Interruption* and on night-time talk shows such as the comedy talk show, *Rove*.

George with Denise Drysdale

George with Bert Newton

George with Rove McManus

George was even interviewed via satellite and phone so he could talk to reporters in other states. Everyone could have a little piece of him. Radio stations such as 2UE in Sydney interviewed George by phone before he even reached the country and Radio 3AW in Melbourne had a Breakfast Show Cook Off to talk up the grill. We even prerecorded a skit with Pluck-a-Duck from *Hey Hey It's Saturday* as George had to fly home and could not appear live on the show. Each time we went to Australia, news of George filled the airways from television, to radio to printed media.

Keep in mind Australia only had three, free major commercial stations in 1999 and no pay-per-view TV channels like they have now. Taped interviews were still not used often and we wanted to make the most of the visits to Australia and be in as many places as George was invited to be. One evening, two talk shows desperately wanted George to be on air with them and they were live to air shows, not pre-recorded, and they aired at the same time.

We didn't feel right selecting one show over the other, and even though they both wanted George exclusively, we struck a deal with each that George would be on one during the first part of the show and on the other during the last half of the show.

We achieved this as the television studios were not far away from each other, so we were rushed, but made it work. The first evening show was called *Live & Kicking*, a comedy show with Australian football players as hosts. The show started with George grilling food just to the side of the audience then he joined the hosts on the main stage for an interview.

I must not have made time in the schedule for a meal break on the day of this shoot. George took the food he had been grilling to the main stage area where he offered snacks to the hosts and ate what must have been his dinner that night as he answered questions from the football players.

After that evening, I made sure to put meal breaks into the schedule so he didn't have to make his own dinner while we were on PR tours. We left the *Live & Kicking* studio, jumped into the car and quickly headed to the other television station studio where George appeared on *The Panel.*

The hosts were a group of 5 Aussie comedians. They sat with George around a round table with the grill and food in the middle; it was the main topic of conversation and George made burgers for the comedians. It was like an infomercial in a whole new format!

This was probably one of the best free advertising hours on Australian TV for us. Anyone flipping channels that evening must have wondered how George managed to be in two places at once given these were both live to air shows.

Another evening show George appeared on was the *110% Tony Squires Show* on Channel 7. This was to me the funniest segment with George down under. George was a full on comedian that night with Tony and the co-hosts. He opened the interview by asking the live audience if anyone wanted to fight, which had everyone in the studio laughing from the start. The host and co-hosts all interacted with George, asking him questions, and he just kept the laughter rolling. Even when they brought out the grill and started cooking, the comedy didn't stop.

We also made store and public appearances where people from miles around came out to meet this American who had landed on their shores. Stores in Australia filled with as many people as we had at events across America, showing us that George's appeal really spread across vast amounts of ocean.

During one visit, we headed to a studio to film a television commercial with Australian 'flavor.' Kebobs cooked up on the grill were one of the features shown for this advertisement. The make-up artist was not so great on that shoot and let's just say that George ended up with very pretty eyes for the camera. No wonder he liked to put on his own camera make up after that.

What would a visit to Australia be without taking in a 'real' football match? One evening we went to the Melbourne Cricket Ground to see a 'footy' match. Channel 7 was airing the game and George was interviewed on the field by Robert DiPierdomenico, known as The Big Dipper, an Australian football legend. Richmond was playing, so we popped a Tigers team scarf around George's neck and sewed a Lean Mean Fat Reducing Grilling Machine patch onto a beanie he was wearing. George can totally adapt to any situation and being with the Aussie footballers was no exception.

We reached a whole new Australian fan base.

During press conferences, not only was the media invited, but also the retail buyers, Australian Olympiads and even Gus Mercurio, a former boxer himself. We pulled George this way and that to introduce him to everyone in the room so everybody went home with a great memory and usually an autograph, photo and a story or interview to tell their friends, family or readers about.

When George sat down and spoke with Aussie Olympiads, they would share stories of the Olympics and their medal wins. When George met Gus, it was amazing to see these two greats together. Though they lived on different continents, their business relationships with Leon created a commonality and bond. I made a call back to the USA and put Gus on the phone with Leon as a surprise to both of them. As the song goes, it's a small world after all.

George Foreman with Brooke Hanson; Australian Olympic Medalist

George with Gus Mercurio

It wasn't all work, although the days and nights were hectic. One afternoon, as George was with his son, George III, I gave him a break so father and son could see some Australian native animals. We headed to Featherdale Wildlife Park outside of Sydney. George and George III were able to feed kangaroos and emus, hold snakes and koalas and talk to a kookaburra. The staff was wonderful and the other tourists were in awe of the extra attractions they got to see that day with an American celebrity in the park.

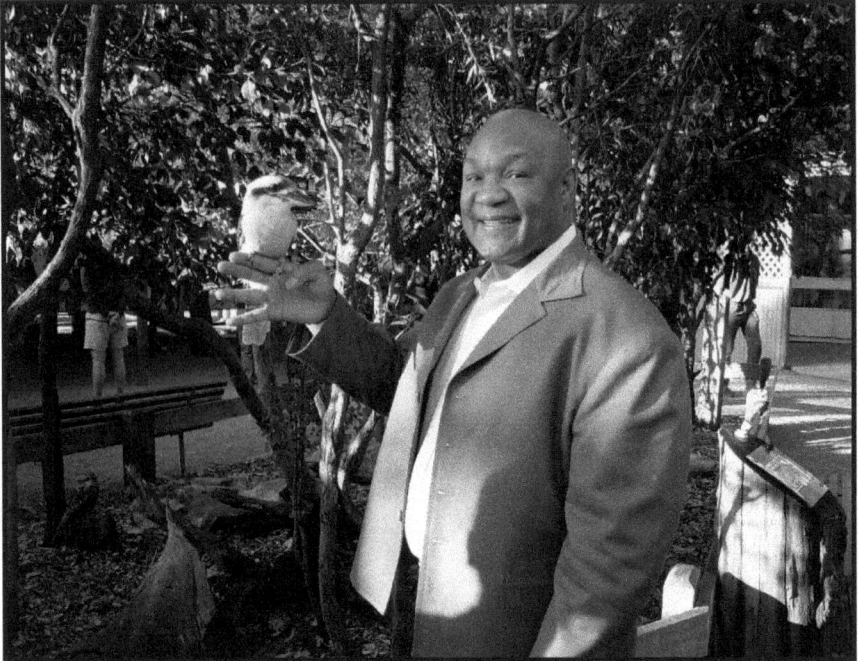

George meets a local Australian at Featherdale Wildlife Park; a Kookaburra

United Kingdom

The grill was a roaring success across North America so with the acquisition of a company in Manchester, Salton was able to take the UK and the rest of Europe by storm in an attempt to repeat the USA success. This set up new travel obstacles. George always had to be home in Texas for Sunday church services, so travel days from Houston were late Sunday night or on a Monday morning and I had to have him home by Saturday nights. I also had to work around Georges HBO commentary schedule at the time.

We were now starting to travel overseas more often and cover several countries in one trip. George's PR schedules became extremely busy. George didn't get a lot of sleep but he just kept on smiling, telling his stories and selling. He would arrive early in the morning into London and I would whisk him off to his first interview of the day, usually on the radio, so we could catch the commuters listening on their way to work.

Sometimes these interviews started in the car by phone or with a reporter joining us for the ride to our first location. Often, George didn't get to see his hotel room until much later on the arrival day and usually that was so he could grab some lunch and freshen up for the afternoon interviews, which were generally with magazine and newspaper reporters. In the evenings it was time to hit the late night talk show circuit.

Between 2001 and 2006, George and the grill took the European media circuit by storm, appearing on a variety of talk and sports shows such as *Something for the Weekend, CNN, Bloomberg* and *Sky Sports, The Frank Skinner Show, Stephan Raab* and *Friday Night with Jonathon Ross*, just to name a few. Articles appeared in UK magazines and newspapers such as *Men's Fitness, Now, Beautiful Kitchens, Fresh, The Times, The People, Prima, ERT, Celebs on Sunday, The Observer* and many more.

We visited radio stations or spoke to DJ's by phone for radio interviews with BBC *Five Live*, BBC *Radio 1*, *Radio 5 Live*, *Saga 1052*, *Talk Sport*, *Virgin* and *XFM* as well as all the others, of whom there are too many to list. George was even interviewed on the radio with people like *DJ Vernon Kay* who grilled, live on the radio. A grill was set up at the radio station and the DJ and George cooked. This was before many radio stations starting filming their segments for the web so the visuals were more for added audio entertainment and photo opportunities.

One of the most memorable interviews of all time for me was when George appeared on the *Frank Skinner show* in London in 2002. The BBC in the UK has all sorts of rules about product placement on television so the producers and our UK PR team were really put to the creative test.

We were there, after all, to make sure the word of the grill was spread far and wide, but BBC rules made that a challenge. Frank Skinner is incredibly funny and very clever. He started out talking to George about the grill and showed the product, but in accordance to BBC rules, the segment couldn't look like an advertisement. They then discussed boxing and clever Frank threw in grill references throughout the interview about George's boxing career.

The show ended with George and Frank singing and dancing to *Let's Twist Again* and two grills were set up to the side of the stage with microphones held up to them and someone making the lids open and close with invisible string so it looked like the grills were backup singers.

This was truly brilliant and a creative way of showing the grill. This was also when I learned that George could sing and dance. I heard rumors that the show was fined by the BBC for this stunt, but hopefully that was just a rumor.

During one UK visit, George created a traffic jam in Harrods as we made our way to the basement following a chap dressed up in a kilt and playing the bag pipes. There was noise, there was chaos, there were so many fans and slam bang in the middle, there we were, wondering what was going on and where they were leading us. Even in London, the fans lined up for the chance to meet George and take home the proof of their meeting. This boxer and Olympiad was a celebrity far and wide.

George Foreman in Harrods, London, United Kingdom

We made numerous visits to the UK over the years and George's celebrity and grill sales just kept growing. Not only did we visit London, we also made our way to Manchester so George could visit the Salton office there and meet the staff he hadn't met in London. We also met with even more reporters. It was always good for staff morale when George met the team behind the sales and marketing efforts in the USA and in every country we visited. This was a team effort and everyone knew it.

During one of our last promotional tours in Europe, we were met by a taxi emblazoned with the grill, George's face and the product name on it. This taxi spent most of the week with us taking some of the team to various events we had scheduled around the city. On the way back to Heathrow, London's airport, we stopped at a truck stop to see a semi trailer carrying the grills. The truck was also covered with the grill branding. To passers-by, this would have been a funny image. George at a truck stop in what looked like the middle of nowhere, taking photos with a trailer with his face and name on it. Even to me, it was a funny image and in true English form, it was drizzling. We got our photo op in and were a bit damp.

London Cab Promotion

Truck used to transport and deliver grills to retailers across the United Kingdom

Each country had their unique press relations team working on new and unusual ways to promote the brand. The UK was no exception. The press conference in 2006 was held in Trafalgar Square in central London with Lord Nelson's Column in the background. Not only could the press watch a cooking demonstration and meet George, the public could also take a gander at the new product being launched that year. The sun was shining, photo-opportunities included George and the grill and Lord Nelson and once again, I was impressed by how creative the teams were in the ways they promoted the grill and conducted press events.

Another memorable late night talk show appearance in the UK was when George appeared on the *Graham Norton Show.* The PR group also got creative in how they got the grill on air and got around the shows fear of the BBC rules regarding product placement and blatant on-air advertising. They wrapped up a grill in pink wrapping paper as a gift for George to give to Graham. Before George went on stage, we handed him the grill and asked him to give it to Graham when the time was right. George didn't ask any questions, he just followed our prompts and directions.

George got a plug in with the product name whilst he raised an eye brow to the audience for fear of being bleeped. I had warned him, we were not allowed to look like we were 'advertising' anything, so he tried to be careful. He then handed Graham the wrapped gift. One of the other guests asked if it was a pink grill. Sure enough, Graham unwrapped the gift and it was a pink grill. Given Graham is exuberantly gay, the pink grill was a little tongue-in-cheek on our part. Graham and the other guests loved it.

For those who haven't seen Graham's late night talk show, it is a wonderfully funny, British-style humor weekly show. George was able to join in on the fun with his very expressive facial reactions and one liners, which got laughs all round, although I occasionally cringed whilst watching from the green room when I knew the humor was not in good taste for our preacher from Texas.

Graham added another grill plug by making reference to Salton UK's campaign to raise over 300,000 pounds for the British Heart Foundation. The BHF and Salton UK asked people to submit a healthy grill recipe together with an optional donation to the BHF. In return, a winner was selected each month and winners received a grill with removable plates and a chance to win £1000.

UK PR for BHR

Graham Norton, George Foreman, Elaine Paige, Ed Byrne and Griff Rhys-Jones

Immediate Release

GEORGE FOREMAN SWAPS BOXING GLOVES FOR OVEN GLOVES AS HE GIVES UK A GRILLING!

HeavyWeight Launches Fundraising Partnership with the British Heart Foundation

George Foreman is in London this month to celebrate the 10 year anniversary of the lean, mean, fat reducing grilling machine. To mark the success, a three-year fundraising partnership with the British Heart Foundation (BHF) has been announced.

George has teamed up with the nation's heart charity with the aim of raising at least £300,000 for pioneering research that saves and improves the lives of vulnerable adults and children. To celebrate the fundraising knockout, he will officially launch the fundraising partnership and demonstrate some of his favourite healthy recipes by swapping the boxing gloves for oven gloves and cooking live in Trafalgar Square (on Friday 20 October at 11am) on his lean, mean, fat-reducing grilling machine. The recipes cooked are featured in the free cook book that comes with all BHF fundraising-branded grills.

This partnership will help raise vital funds for the BHF, so it can continue its research into the causes and treatments for heart disease.

George's passionate approach to healthy living has turned the legendary sportsman from successful boxer to businessman, with over ten million grills sold in the UK alone since its launch, he's clearly appealing to different generations, bringing the convenience factor to healthy eating.

UK Press Release

George was invited to be a guest on *Friday Night with Jonathon Ross*. The show is set up with a faux green room where the guests for the evening sit together and a camera pans the area to show who will be on the show. I say "faux green room" as there were no walls, just a section off the main stage with a couple of couches and a table so camera crew can easily film the area.

George and I were in this 'room' and up walks Paul McCartney, no entourage in sight. George introduced me to this famous Beatle and after I said hello, I became somewhat lost for words. We were sitting down on the couches, just the three of us, and a cameraman came swinging by every now and then. My mind was working overtime thinking things like, *his vegan shoes look pretty good* and *I bet my Mom would love to be sitting in my place right now*.

George and Paul chatted away to each other like old friends; they had met before.

I wondered if I should say something. All I could come up with was, "I was given your White Album for my 16th birthday." Well, you won't believe what Paul's reply was. He said, "You must be really old." I was 34 years old and had just been insulted by a Beatle. I still laugh about this.

All was forgiven when Paul took his turn to be interviewed by Jonathon Ross and told everyone how much he liked George's grill; a plug on primetime national television by Paul McCartney. Does it get any better?

Over the years, the number of celebrities who spoke about their love of the grill during national television interviews grew and grew; we couldn't have been happier or more surprised. Celebrities such as Noah Wiley who was starring in ER at the time gave a great plug on Leno about buying the grill off the infomercial and how it was on a slant and fat dripped into the trays. It actually became so common place that after a while it barely fazed us when celebrities spoke about how great the grill was.

When in London, we always stayed at the Lanesborough Hotel. During one of our stays, out of the corner of my eye, I kept seeing a short man, dressed in an 1800s green velvet jump suit, just laying on the chaise lounge, on his side, perched up on his elbow with his hand holding up his head. This was just outside of the far left elevator. I saw this man for a couple of days in a row. A man who wasn't actually there when I looked directly at the seat.

Once I was sure my jet lag had subsided and I was sure I wasn't 'seeing things', I asked the staff at the front desk if anyone else had reported seeing someone in the lobby who wasn't really there and I described who I had seen. The staff wasn't the least bit phased by my question. They explained that the hotel was formerly St. George's Hospital, built in the 1800s and converted into a hotel in the late 20th century.

There had been several ghost sightings over the years and the hotel was part of a local haunted tours attraction that went around London. I had no idea and was also a bit relieved. A few days later I was dining in the hotel restaurant with Leon. I was sitting in a high back chair situated in an area where no one could walk behind me. I felt someone touch their hand on my shoulder and asked Leon if there was anyone behind me. There wasn't.

I loved this hotel ghosts and all. It was one of my favorite hotels to stay in during promotional tours and the staff were amazing.

Unfortunately the hotel has undergone renovations so the grandeur of the original Lanesborough Hotel has been sold off at auction but I do hope to experience the modern version of it one day and hopefully catch a glimpse of my friendly ghost again.

George in London. UK Press Conference.

EUROPE

As part of taking Europe by storm, not only did we focus PR efforts in the UK, George traveled to Germany, Italy, Spain, Belgium, Ireland and France, often visiting several countries within a 5-day period. Whether we had to fly or drive long distances, we covered as much ground as we could.

We learned early on during a visit to Europe that the right translator made all the difference in the world if you are to have a great interview in a foreign language. At first, some of our translators did just that; translated the words but not the feeling. George tells jokes and funny stories so we had to find translators who were skilled in interpreting the words with the intended feelings and it made all the difference in the world to the end result.

In Germany, as well as the usual press conference and media events, George appeared on QVC there. George already had QVC experience after many hours on-air in the USA and also on QVC in the UK. We were now on the German version of the show, the format was the same, but the show was in German and the show host had to talk in German and help George and get him involved. The host also spoke in English to bring George into the sales pitch. George managed to do what he does best, ad lib and eat cooked food straight off the grill whilst the host went back and forth in two languages. Seeing George eat food off the grill was always a big hit with audiences everywhere.

During one visit to Germany, George's daughter Natalie was with us. We visited a department store where a radio program had set up their DJ booth on the retail floor so George could be interviewed in front of a live audience. We also went to a radio station studio where the host cooked on the grill for listeners and he taught Natalie to say, "My father is king of the grill," in German so she could say it on the air and be a part of the show. *Mein Vater ist der König von der Grill.* George kept laughing whilst his daughter was a good sport and had her German lesson. The people we encountered in Hamburg and across Germany were delightful and a lot of fun.

We also had the opportunity to visit Cologne where George was a guest on the *Stefan Raab Show* in 2005 and again in 2006. This is an evening talk show with a live audience and what must be "German humor." Stefan was brilliant in talking back and forth between English and German to keep George and his audience involved. He also has a lot of enthusiasm which showed as he bounced around the stage. During the 2006 episode, live chickens were on the set and as it turned out, this wasn't going to be the last time we had George sharing a stage with live chickens.

Stefan and George sat down and got the basic interview questions out of the way. Then, after a commercial break they came back on air to cook. Several grills were set up on stage, warming up and ready to go. Stefan popped on a chef's hat and they both put on their aprons to start grilling. George sets out to do a serious cooking demonstration as he likes to cook and show what the grill can do. Stefan, on the other hand, puts a German dessert of chocolate covered marshmallows on a grill and closes the lid. George just looks at him quizzically and continues to grill 'normal food.'

When Stefan opened his grill lid, I must admit, the melted dessert actually looked pretty good. Things then got a little weird as George continued to grill his food and sell the product's features and Stefan pulls out small, plastic Smurf® dolls and tries to grill them.

Then, Stefan followed the Smurfs® with a Barbie® doll, which George eventually rescued off the grill to the sound of the audience gushing at how sweet it was for this big boxer to take Barbie® off the grill and away from Stefan. The 'Awwwws' from the audience needed no translation.

To finish the skit, the host put a mobile cellular phone on the grill and tried to melt it, but delighted in the fact that it kept ringing after being cooked. George kept his composure throughout the crazy segment and didn't miss a beat in demonstrating the grill and keeping up with this bizarre show hosts antics.

George Foreman and Stefan Raab

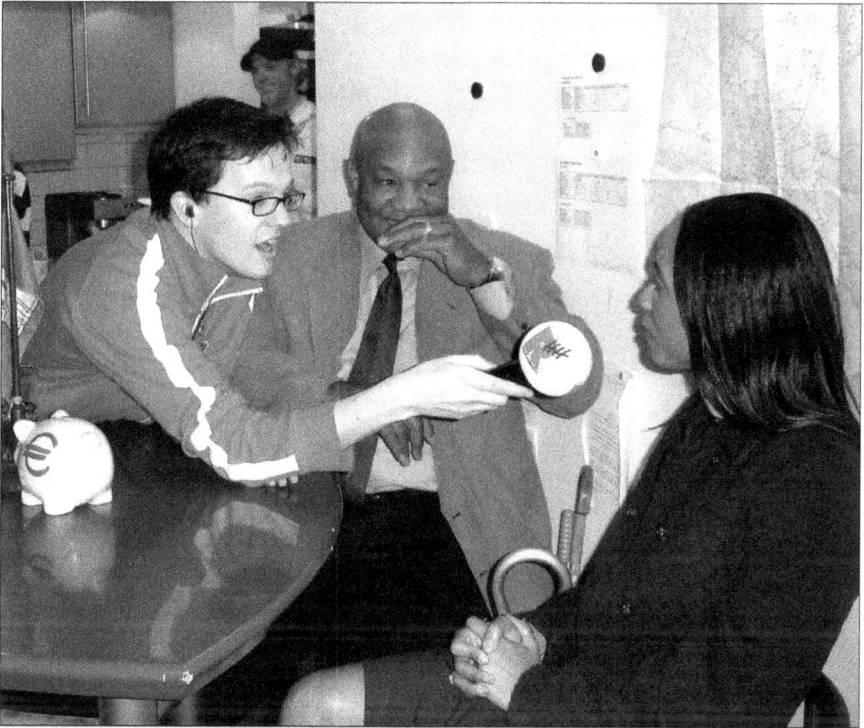

Germany with Natalie Foreman

No matter what situation he found himself in around the world, Big George adapted to local ways, humor and whatever was thrown at him, even when he was sleep deprived and didn't speak the language. In some interviews, I could see his eyes were red and dark circles were forming as he hadn't slept or was jet-lagged, but he didn't complain and just kept working; a true professional every step of the way, unafraid of hard work.

In Belgium, a local company called Princess, was responsible for selling the grill in their region and once again PR efforts catered to the local market. They also wanted to do what they could to welcome an American to their homeland; so it was an interesting press conference to say the least.

We stayed in Amsterdam and drove to Belgium for the press conference; it was a relatively short drive away. We were greeted by girls dressed in American style-cheerleader outfits who gave George a cheer as we entered the historic building rented for the event. George raised one eyebrow at me, wondering what country I said we were in. This was a look I got very accustom to over the years.

I was as floored as he was by the welcome reception. Once inside, there were introductions, cooking demonstrations, speeches and George once again gave me a sideways glance that this time I interpreted as, 'help me figure out what is going on,' as he was serenaded by a lady singing to him in her native tongue whilst someone played the piano. All I could do was laugh to myself whilst George fidgeted on the stool and just kept smiling. It was probably the most unusual press conference and retail buyer event we had ever encountered.

Belgium Cheerleader Welcome

Belgium with the Princess Team

SOUTH AFRICA

We had purchased the majority of shares in a local South African Company called Amalgamated Appliances, or AMAP as they were known, so in 2003 we headed to Johannesburg to launch the grill.

George sat in a room for hours and hours as reporters lined up to photograph and interview him, some speaking Afrikaans for whom we had to find a translator. He always had a smile and a tale to tell no matter how long he sat there.

He answered the same questions over and over in the windowless room. You can imagine how interested sports reporters were to talk to the man with the reputation as the mean guy from the *Rumble in the Jungle* days when he fought in Zaire nearly 30 years before and how surprised they were by this friendly salesman in front of them. Reporters writing about health topics and general interest stories were consumed by tales of the grill. Many asked George for his favorite recipe or cooking tips they could print for their column.

Newspaper articles appeared during the following weeks, some in sports sections of newspapers such as *This Day, Saturday Star* and *Daily News*. Interviews were also featured in Special Interest sections of newspapers such as *The Sunday Metro Times*, who listed "The Top Ten Tips from George" about cooking, including the tip to add color to your meals with vegetables and to experiment so things don't get boring.

During the following months after George's visit to Johannesburg, stories from the man, his grill and his life as well as snippets about the new healthy cooking appliances including the George Foreman Rotisserie and Outdoor Grill could be found in periodicals such as *People, Wine and Food, Elle, Sunflyer* and *Extra Mile Magazine, Drum, FHM, SA 4x4, Getaway, Sarie, Caravan, Outdoor Life* and many more.

We also made an in-store appearance in Johannesburg. The store was filled with balloons and streamers. Grills lined the aisles and security was present in plain sight to control the crowd, if necessary. Mothers were there with their children, men were there on their lunch breaks. No one was causing any trouble. Everyone was just happy to be there, to get their photographs taken with George and receive personalized autographs; some even bought a grill.

During this visit, we were given word that Nelson Mandela had made a request to meet George. The local office was ecstatic and wanted to come along in hopes of getting a glimpse of their national hero and to make sure a grill was given to him; it was.

We made our way to Mandela's headquarters, where we were greeted by security. George, George, George's nephew and I were allowed to enter the sacred ground, so to speak. Security was tight. I sat there listening to Mandela and George as they shared boxing stories and spoke about other celebrities who had sat where we were now. A photographer waited outside to capture this moment in history.

Here were two men whose earlier years of struggle as younger men were far behind them; they could have turned into bitter, older men but instead, had cheerful positive demeanors; role models for their countries and the world.

Mandela's people would only allow one photographer of their choosing to photograph the men as we were leaving the building. I stood aside so these two gents could have a photo opportunity, but Mandela grabbed my arm to pull me into the photo session.

He may have been an older, somewhat frail looking chap, but he had a grip on him that gave me some insight as to the tough guy he was when he was younger. He was also so thoughtful that he wanted to make sure I was in the photos with him and George.

The downside of the story, however, is when I tried to get a copy of the photos from the photographer. He met me at the hotel and asked for cash to get the photos developed, then he would drop them off to me the next day. I had no reason not to trust him as he was the 'chosen' photographer, so I gave him the cash. Well, that was an expensive lesson.

This photographer failed to show up with the prints and made excuse after excuse on the phone as to why he couldn't get them to me. I still feel silly and ripped off to this day as the photos never showed up and I know they exist as I saw a proof sheet. Luckily someone from AMAP snapped a few shots so I do have an unposed memento from the day which shows I was there.

A photo of Mandela play punching at a smiling George appeared in the *Saturday Star* and *Daily Sport* newspapers.

George Foreman and Nelson Mandela

George Foreman, George Dumas, Nelson Mandela and
Samantha Dreimann

BRAZIL

In 2003, after launching the grill in Europe, we headed to South America where I was able to see George's dancing prowess again. Given the language barrier, television commercial advertising was a new challenge if it was to include George. In Brazil we worked with one of the best crews I have come across in the world. They created a commercial which mostly includes George chopping vegetables to the sound of upbeat music. He is shown grilling, then finishes off the spot doing the Samba whilst a voice-over does the rest. Yes, George doing the Samba to sell the grill.

I was on the other side of the set behind the camera also doing the Samba so George could copy my hand movements and have a good laugh as well I am sure, as I tried to figure out the correct moves for him to make. We were in a very small, nondescript warehouse with a very small crew, yet it is one of the best commercials for the grill ever produced.

A second 30-second spot was filmed in Brazil which included a local celebrity who shows up at someone's front door with George and a grill. They are invited into the kitchen to show the lady of the house the new product.

In each country we visited, we did promotions in and shot commercials in and for, we were always conscious to adapt to the local ways and needs, rather than asking them to adapt to us. This truly assisted in the sales and acceptance of this American household name product and brand around the world.

Being that we were in Brazil where locals are known to enjoy a night out, the grill launch was at an evening party where all the retail buyers and several media channels were invited to meet George, see the product in action and to socialize. Retail buyers, no matter what country we were in, always loved it when they could meet the Champ, shake his hand and have photos taken to prove this happened.

Later that evening, on the way back to the hotel, in our bullet proof car, (yes, the manager of the local office insisted we needed this type of protection), we drove down a street lined with 'ladies of the night.'

George, once again being a gentleman and showing his preacher side, spoke about his concern for the young ladies being out on the street so late at night. I wasn't sure if I should respond, but I thought it best to point out that those ladies were actually men dressed as women on the street, just trying to earn a living and they could probably take care of themselves. There was silence in the car.

If we had of thought to film all of the behind the scenes events during these press tours we would have been able to make a very funny reality television show out of the footage.

During our time in Brazil, George was interviewed by all the local media from newspapers to magazines to appearing on the most famous daytime talk show, the host of which appeared in a commercial with him.

The local office got creative on how to promote the grill and followed the idea that worked in Australia with the van. Only the van grew into a traveling truck decorated with images of George, the grill and the branding messages. The truck was specially fitted with a kitchen and access was made to consumers to see the grill being demonstrated. This truck travelled to shopping centers around the country and to more rural areas where the response was always positive and more and more grill sales were made.

In some cities, we made stops that were not media related, but helped the community we were visiting. George was asked to visit a youth center which had a boxing ring and helped keep kids off the street. This sort of place was right up George's alley as boxing had helped him as a young man. He too had opened a youth and community center in Texas to help keep local youth busy after school, on weekends and during the holiday seasons.

Due to crazy traffic in the city in Brazil, and how many hours it would have taken us to cross town, we took an elevator to the top of a tall building and jumped into a helicopter to make our way quickly to the youth center. It wasn't bullet proof, but it was an interesting mode of transport to make our way to see the kids. One of the gentlemen from the youth center met us at the landing pad and escorted us to the center.

The kids eyes lit up like lights on a Christmas tree when George walked through the door. They were thrilled to meet a boxing legend. George did one of the things he does best. He spoke to these young people about life and taking the right path to be good in this world. He inspired them to be all that they could be and take the high road as best they could.

George's nephew George was with us on this day and I asked him what the smell was in the gym. I understood his reply, Southern accent and all. "Sam, that's sweat." Now when I smell something not right, I recall that moment.

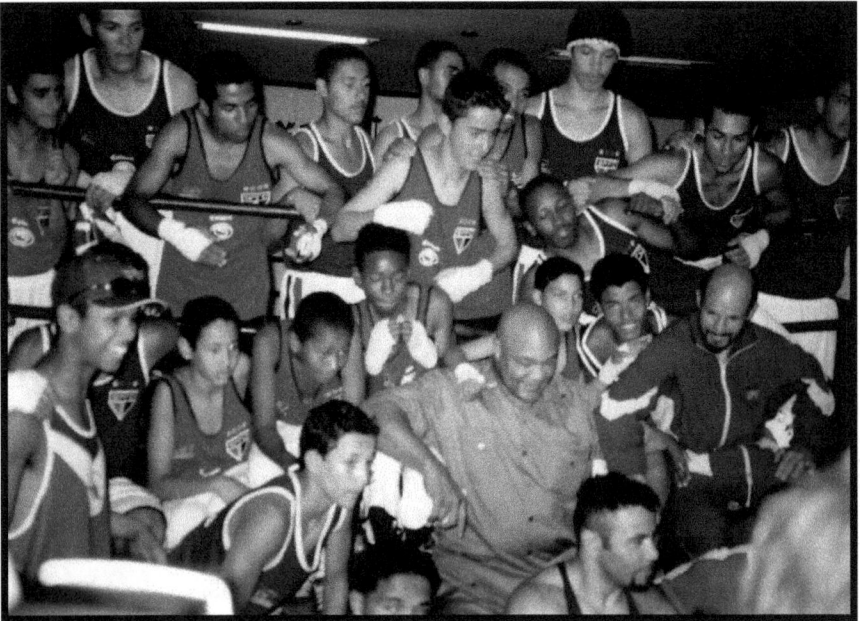

George visiting a Youth Center in Brazil

DUBAI

We had taken North America, Europe, Australia and South America by storm. If residents in those countries did not know of George and the grill, then they must not have watched television or opened a newspaper or magazine in years. It was now time to spread the word of healthy grilling to the Middle East. What better launching pad for this than Dubai? It was 2007 and Dubai had been the talk of the world with its' explosion of wealth and construction as far as the eyes could see.

Our Hong Kong office partnered with Jashanmal Group's consumer division to launch the grill across the Middle East. Jashanmal had the infrastructure and connections to get the grill into as many retailers and homes as possible in the region and they did just that.

Before George arrived in Dubai, I set out to get a lay of the land. I wanted to understand the people and the culture and to know what we could expect when talking to the retailers and the press there.

Bert Doornmalen from our Hong Kong office drove me to nearly every mall across the city and it quickly became apparent that I was in a place where people liked to shop more than Americans did. These were not just basic strip malls and shopping centers, these were wildly extravagant shopping plazas, each with their own theme and each an exercise work out to get from one end to the other.

When George and his son George III arrived, our hosts from Jashanmal arranged for us to take a helicopter tour over the city to see all the construction and get a bird's eye view of the homes being erected on islands which were being built out at sea.

With all the interviews and meetings lined up for the following days, George was able to talk firsthand about what he had seen from the air and tell the story of how his breath had been taken away high in the sky. It was amusing to see George and his son's reaction to the city, as they seemed to truly love what they saw and were like big kids who enjoyed seeing construction sites. Boys will be boys.

Store visits were arranged and the usual autograph signing sessions saw people from far and wide line up to meet the Champ. We entered the Mercato Shopping Center where George made a presentation on the main stage. Then we sat George down in Spinneys, a leading supermarket chain in Dubai where the aisles were lined with grills, and George's fans lined up for the meet and greet session. We also made an appearance at the Jashanmal Department Store where George signed his cookbooks and even packaging that the grills came in. With so many shops and fans in Dubai, we could have stayed there for a month and been kept busy with PR. We even made a pre-arranged visit to an airport Duty Free store which was stocked high with grills.

Making our way through tight security at the airport proved a little challenging as I got in trouble for having a small camera with me. I am not sure what the issue was, but the local agents had to talk the security guards out of taking me away. That was a close call. I don't think I would have fared well in a Dubai jail cell.

We attended an ABC (American Business Council of Dubai and North America) luncheon that honored George as their guest. They wanted to figure out the key to his success in business. The ABC is a chapter of the Chamber of Commerce with over 600 members comprising of American business and individual members. It is one of the largest business councils in Dubai, having been around for over 30 years now.

The objective of the ABC is to promote the development of commerce and investment between the USA and the United Arab Emirates. It isn't often they have a guest such as George, so there wasn't an empty seat in the ballroom for this special luncheon.

Jashanmal hosted a "Dinner with the Champion" in the ballroom of the Jumeirah Beach Hotel, for a select group of several hundred VIP's including Chef Osama, retail buyers and distributors from across the Middle East.

There had been a competition for chefs to prepare meals on the grills with 20 finalists being invited to cook at the VIP event where the competition continued. Local chefs, mostly from the high end hotels and restaurants in the city, were stationed around the room preparing food on grills to show off the products' capabilities and also as part of the continuing competition. Five winners were announced at the end of the night and awarded prizes and certificates presented to them by George. There were speeches, awards, photo opportunities and of course, lots of food.

George with chefs in Dubai at Jashanmal's VIP event

The press conference was held at the Emirates Mall which has the first of its kind indoor ski slope in the world. A restaurant called Apres was rented out for the day and a stage was erected where George, assisted by a local chef, grilled for the audience with a back drop of 3000 square meters of snow.

While George grilled, he told stories and answered questions. People behind him on the slopes skied and made their way down the hill on toboggans. George told one of his stories about losing the fight against Ali in Zaire because he ate a fat laden cheese burger before the match and that he won the heavy weight title back at 45 years of age because he still ate burgers, but this time cooked on the grill without all the fat. He finishes this story by telling everyone they are crazy if they believe him, but it is a great story to get people's attention and a laugh.

Media interviews were arranged with every major and minor newspaper such as *Emirates Evening Post, Telelife, Aquarius, Inside Out, OK, Emirates Home, Living in the Gulf* as well as periodicals such as *Time Out Dubai, Arabian Business, Total Sport, Gulf Gourmet, Charged* and many more. Everyone sent a reporter to talk to George.

Even radio stations sent out their crews to our location for the now popular, cooking on the radio air waves segments with George. Television news crews such as *City 7 News* and *Asia Net* filmed at the VIP dinner and *Zee TV* showed clips of George grilling at the press conference.

Articles and cover stories showed up in over 100 media channels and we had only been in Dubai for three days. Some of the media headlines after the interviews with George were creative such as, *"From Killer to Griller," "Knockout," "The Legendary Champ," "Grilled; George Foreman turns up the heat on Dubai,"* and possibly my favorite, *"Gorgeous George."*

The most memorable television appearance in Dubai was when George appeared on the *Chef Osama* cooking show. Chef Osama has an audience of millions of viewers across several continents. He currently has over a million likes on Facebook so that will give you an idea of his own celebrity status.
http://www.chefosama.com/

Osama, born in Egypt, had spent a great deal of time in America where he studied, earned the designation of Certified Executive Chef and has done such things as serve up his fine cuisine for political dignitaries such as former US President, Bill Clinton and former Vice President, Al Gore.

Given Chef Osama's background in America and the Middle East, he easily cooked up local Middle Eastern dishes using the George Foreman grill and had a set that was wall to wall food. There was even a very large prop camel in the background.

This was one of the most colorful sets I have ever seen for a cooking show. George and Osama cooked up an array of dishes on the kitchen set, to the delight of the viewers. They both got along splendidly well. Once the cameras stopped rolling, George and George III set about to chow down on the tantalizing dishes that had been created on the show. Based on the smiles on their faces, I do believe this was the best food they had whilst in Dubai.

To finish our time in Dubai, George wanted to see and walk on the sand dunes. Our driver that day was puzzled when I asked him to drop George and his son off in the middle of the sandy desert and drive a little way away so we could wait for the lads to make their way to us. I made sure to keep them in sight, but they looked like ants from where we parked on a sand dune.

There was no one else around; such a peaceful escape from the hustle and bustle of the city under construction. Most tourists want the dune driving experience of being thrown around in the four wheel drive whilst the driver travels over dunes making one feel like they are about to roll. Not George. He wanted to experience the sand beneath his feet and to get some exercise walking over the dunes.

After the desert trek, we stopped to see some camels and somehow George III and I convinced George to take a camel ride. He is accustomed to riding horses, but there was something entertaining about watching George hold on tight to the camel reins.

George on set with Chef Osama in Dubai

George and George III on a camel ride in the desert in Dubai.

HONG KONG

There was a lot of talk about how best to spread the word of George and his grill to the Asian market. This is an area of the globe with millions of people who have a very different palette and way of cooking compared to the Western world. How does one launch an essentially American product used for very western cooking to the eastern world? You talk to your friendly Hollywood attorney who 'knows people.'

Through one of our friends in Los Angeles, CA, a Hollywood attorney, Sam Perlmutter, who had been part of the original grill partnership between George and Salton, a deal was put into motion between the Salton Hong Kong office and Jackie Chan. Yes, Jackie Chan was to be the spokesperson along with George for the grill to have a chance to penetrate the Asian markets.

An impressive team up indeed. A World Heavy-Weight Boxing Champion cooking up a storm with a celebrity martial artist. Visions of an odd couple sprang to mind, but also, what a great team!

These two gentlemen were children born and raised in countries far away from each other. Both came from very simple childhoods where money was scarce and both had made their way through life to fame, fortune and giving back to their communities; such different gentlemen yet alike in many ways.

In April, 2007 we flew to Hong Kong where Jackie and George met, exchanged autographs, and were the stars of a very entertaining press conference at the famous Peninsula Hotel. Both chaps delighted the reporters with charm and wit as they answered all the questions thrown at them. It was like they had known each other for years rather than minutes.

There was a natural chemistry between them or maybe it was just pure professionalism. Whatever it was, this team up worked. In the days following the press conference and the scheduled one-on-one reporter interviews, we filmed the most amazing infomercial that I have ever seen and been witness to behind the scene. It was like a mini movie.

Something like that would never have been filmed in America nor would the infomercial industry in the USA ever be able to create such a great piece of entertainment or believe it would fit into their advertising models. Given this was an Asian production being filmed in Hong Kong with sports heroes who were also actors, the script writers got very creative.

The first thing that took me by surprise when we walked on to the set was the basket of live chickens. Don't worry; no animals were harmed during the making of this infomercial. They were for set decoration only. There were also live crabs and a variety of food that I had only seen in Asian markets, not my local grocery store. The set was decorated with lots of colors and faux food stands representing different Asian countries. The food being grilled needed to appeal to local tastes and that it did.

George and Jackie hammed it up for the cameras as Jackie taught George how to cook local delicacies on the grill. George was a good student and Jackie a good teacher. Jackie juggled on set, he had a fight scene where he showed his acrobatic, martial arts skills and showed us all he could cook really well.

Unfortunately, it was not long after this show was filmed, Salton globally changed hands and management, so we never got to see what could have been done with this infomercial and sales of the grill in China. I am sure it would have been huge, or at the very least, this infomercial would have gone viral and appeared on all social media networks around the world.

On the set in Hong Kong, George Foreman and Jackie Chan

George Foreman, Leon Dreimann, Jackie Chan and Bert Doornmalen

Samantha overseeing the setup during the infomercial filming

Local to Global

I had the pleasure of traveling with and learning from George for over a decade.

No matter where we were, I would always notice George giving a word of encouragement and support for those who needed it, whether we were visiting a boxing gym in Ireland for wayward youth or attending autograph signing sessions in a local shopping center.

There were even times when I would arrange a surprise phone call from George to a fan or someone who needed advice or a pep talk. This made their day.

After sitting in on so many interviews, I was able to answer so many of the reporters standard questions. I really appreciated the reporters who came up with a new question or at least rephrased the standard ones. Yes, the reporters were all polite and made sure to ask about the grill as we were in their country or traveling around the USA promoting the product, but many followed with the same questions:

How many children do you have?
Is it true they are all named George?
Who do you consider to be the greatest boxer?

Then, of course, there were always questions about George's famous match against Muhammad Ali, in Zaire.

The global marketing of the now famous appliance presented by a boxer, turned minister, turned salesman is one for the history books. A truly remarkable pairing of an unlikely product and spokesperson that took the world by storm and was a pleasure to be a part of, not only because of the success story, but to have made so many friends along the way and have an extended family in the way of the Foremans and for the Foremans to have an extended family with us.

From Leon's personal photo collection:
George Foreman visiting our home in Chicago; from left to right, my
daughters, Samantha, Michelle, Alana and my wife, Joy Dreimann.
George was always great with young people and wherever he went
they loved being with him.

RICHARD SIMMONS

I have spoken so much about how the media really got involved with George and the grill publicity, which was all great, but it is worth mentioning that every time one agrees to appear on live media, there is a risk which could be catastrophic.

In 2006, I negotiated a license deal with the effervescent Richard Simmons who was a delight to work with. He had so many fans and helped so many people lose weight over the years, it made sense to create a healthy product with him. Together, we designed a very innovative electric food steamer which could have been the next big thing in the infomercial appliance world. Salton patented the item, had the tooling built, worked with a home economist on a healthy recipe book, invested in inventory and made an infomercial. This was all at a cost that should have paid off significantly.

We traveled to New York, where Richard appeared on several talk shows, demonstrating and spouting the benefits of healthy cooking in the steamer. He made an appearance in the Salton booth at the International Housewares Show in Chicago where people lined up for hugs and his autograph. We were gaining traction, retailers were putting the steamer in their stores and creating end caps for this new, innovative appliance with a well known celebrity and spokesperson on the box.

One day Richard's manager called me to say Richard had been asked to appear on the David Letterman show and asked if I could send them some steamers. Richard and Letterman had a falling out in 2000 when a gag went wrong and resulted in Richard having an asthma attack. Letterman had sprayed Richard in the face with a fire extinguisher. It was time for the late night show host to kiss and make up. Great, we were going to see Richard and the steamer on Letterman.

Well, it turned out to be the worst thing that could have happened. I learned the hard way that some skit writers and show hosts keep their jokes secret and don't think through the consequences of their actions. They also fail to understand, or maybe just don't care, about the harm they can do to a celebrity, the product and financially to the company they scorched. Apologies and retractions come too late. The harm is done. Unbeknownst to Richard, his manager and myself, the show team had turned the steamer into a 'gag'. There was Richard sitting down next to Letterman, talking about his great new product, and Letterman flicks a switch which ignites a flame and sets the steamer on fire. Richard jumps from his chair barely escaping singed hair. Letterman pulls out a fire extinguisher and sprays out the fire, all the time laughing to himself. Not only was this a dangerous and harmful stunt, it wasn't funny. There may have been a handful of people who recalled the 2000 incident and saw the parallels with the fire extinguisher but most did not.

The next day the photo of the steamer on fire was in *The New York Daily Post* and the video clip was the first thing you saw on AOL's home page. My phone was ringing the minute I stepped into my office. Reps, buyers and consumers were concerned about this item malfunctioning and were asking about a recall notice. No matter how many times I tried to explain it was 'a joke' or a 'Letterman stunt' people just saw the product on fire and panicked. Retailers already carrying the product wanted to return it, orders were cancelled. The product had been killed on late night television. The steamer had rave reviews from consumers who got to buy and try it before its demise. It is unfortunate that more people didn't get to experience, Steam Heat™.

Richard Simmons in New York City during Steam Heat™ promotions

Richard Simmons on set in New York City promoting the Steamer

Samantha and Richard Simmons

AFTERWORD BY LEON DREIMANN

I had promised to myself that if we ever sold 100 million grills that I would retire. But did I believe it would ever happen?

So what do you think made this one of the most successful products in the small domestic appliance field?

The most frequent questions I am asked are… How did it happen? Where did you meet George and get the idea to put his name on the grill? What made this simple product so successful? Was the product really that good? Were you lucky? Usually, I give a very short answer, George was fabulous, it is a great product, and I was very lucky! This book may help answer these questions and be useful to current and future entrepreneurs.

Yes, I was very lucky to be introduced to George and get the chance to say let's try to make it happen. Previous experience with celebrities helped a lot. Great relationships with our suppliers brought the product to us instead of a competitor. I had great partners in David Sabin and Bill Rue who supported me 100% and had as much faith in our eventual success as I did.

David Sabin motivated and guided our fabulous sales force, led by our National Sales Managers Keith Hamden, Michael Miller and Robert Schwartz.

Bill Rue built a team to handle our warehousing and distribution to cope with unbelievable growth. I remember one day when our warehouse in California had trucks lined up for two miles for arriving and departing grills to our customers. Can you picture this scene?

As President, Bill was also responsible for building a financial team capable of handling systems to cope with growth that took our company from $8 million in sales to $1.4 billion. He dealt with our banks to get enough money to buy the goods and finance the receivables; not an easy task.

Our grill factory was a seven million square foot facility and we were their biggest customer. For us, they were our biggest supplier. Fully integrated for Die Casting, Injection Molding, Metal Stamping, Tool Making, Packaging Production and of course, assembly. There were days that you stood on the balcony at one end of the factory and saw assembly lines as far as the eyes could see, all making grills, over 10,000 people on assembly lines alone.

Assembly lines at Tsann Kuen in Xiamen, China Xiamen, China

Tsann Kuen in Xiamen, China Xiamen, China

Our creative and exciting marketing team was led by Barbara Alonge as Marketing Director. Barbara Westfield was responsible to oversee our TV Infomercial production, Marketing Campaigns and Product Graphics and Packaging.

You've read Samantha's contribution. Then, there was a young exciting group of product managers being creative with product ideas and marketing in many of the housewares categories.

Our board had the patience to let us persevere with George and the grill when things looked like we could fail.

Then, there was my other partner I have known since my days in Australia, Bert Doornmalen. He built a team in Hong Kong that managed all quality control for production with our suppliers and handled logistics for shipping as many as 15,000 containers in some months to all our branches around the world. Visualize that picture!

Bert loves sales and making deals too. He led the campaign to launch the grill with George and Jackie Chan in China, he found a team to launch the grill in Dubai and the Middle East, and he put us together with AMAP, a company in South Africa that we made a very profitable and successful investment in. He sold grills to our troops in Iraq and found distributors for the grill in Vietnam and Thailand as well as many other markets in Asia.

Bert Doornmalen

Milton Dickins, my CFO with Goldair® almost 40 years ago, was incredible in starting a branch in Australia from scratch and building the business to a very profitable $60 million in a very short time. He has incredible stories to tell of what needed to be done to have us get a foot in retail doors in Australia.

Milton Dickins

Martin Burns, who after 20 years as Managing Director for Morphy Richards® small electrics, applied to be the managing director of our newly acquired Pifco® Company in the UK. Pifco's® major brands included Russell Hobbs® and Salton®. During the interview, when I asked him why he would want to come and work for us as he was already the head of the market leader in the UK, he said you guys look like you may be about to get pretty hot, so I may not be able to beat you. I might as well join you.

He put a great team together in the UK that created many successful products we sold all over the world. With a strong CFO, he then put teams together in Spain, Germany and Italy and launched our brands from a zero business base. Italy did close after a couple of years, but Germany and Spain did well. He also recommended and got approval to buy a small company in France that gave us a base there.

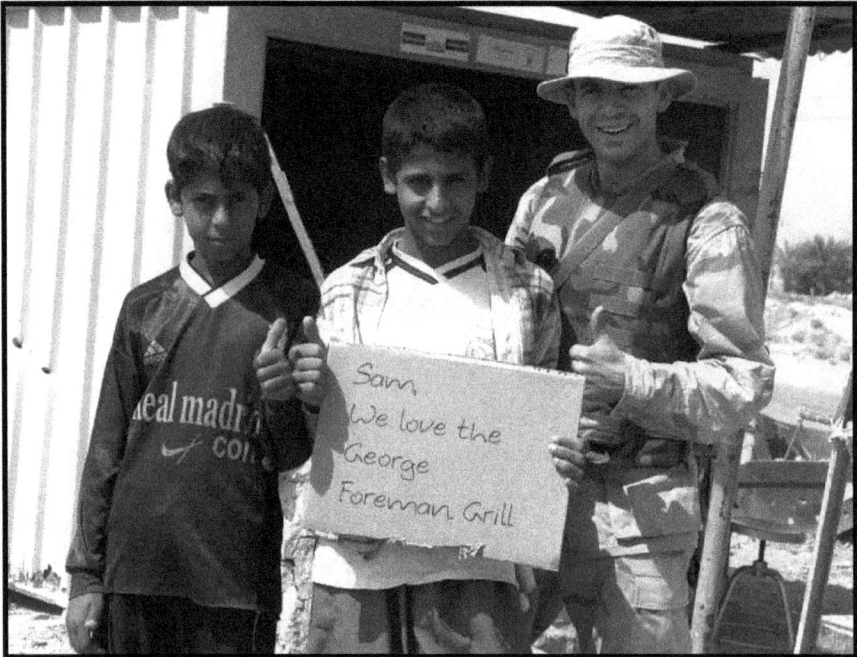

Photo courtesy of Sam Perlmutter

Some members of the Salton team celebrating Barbara Alonge's birthday (third from the left second row). Back row middle is George Foreman Jr. , George's oldest son who was part of our invincible team. Left second row is Keith Hamden, our National Sales Manager, who had the tough job allocating grills without upsetting valuable customers. Second from the right middle row is Jack Hira our amazing Purchasing Manager who kept product flow coming.

There was a wonderful team in South Africa and so many more in the USA and around the rest of the world who helped make this such an incredible story. Sorry, I cannot name you all, but thank you. I was lucky to build a Dream Team for the housewares industry who was loyal to the company and me.

I thank them all and thank the thousands of other people I could not mention here. Many of us still keep in touch and some of us continue to do business together. The one thing we all agree on is… it was fun and exciting to be part of the Salton team for over 20 years.

When a hedge fund company called Harbinger bought the company and merged it with Applica and later merged again with Spectrum, most of the dream team left immediately, the rest within a short period afterwards. George decided he would not extend his contract to make new ads or travel to promote the product. He was loyal to the dream team and once they were gone, he did other things.

For more information and stories follow us on Facebook:
facebook.com/TheArtOfSalesMarketingAndTheSpokesperson

Subscribe to our YouTube Channel:
http://bit.ly/YouTubeTAOSAM

Put us in your Google Circles:
google.com/+TheArtofSalesMarketing

Follow us on Instagram:
http://instagram.com/artofsalesmarketing/

Follow us on Twitter
http://www.twitter.com/TAOSMATS

Contact:
samantha@greystonebrands.com

www.ingramcontent.com/pod-product-compliance
Lightning Source LLC
Chambersburg PA
CBHW060025210326
41520CB00009B/1006